SUBTERRANEAN STOCKPORT

EMMA BROWN

AMBERLEY

This book is dedicated to the memory of Jim Clare – veteran of the Cheshire Regiment, painter, window-cleaner, postal worker, Heritage Trust volunteer, Stockport Town Crier, tour guide, raconteur and great friend. Jim helped with, and followed the progress of, my adventures. I am honoured to have earned from him a nickname, 'Down Under', and hope to continue to live up to it.

First published 2016

Amberley Publishing, The Hill, Stroud
Gloucestershire GL5 4EP

www.amberley-books.com

British Library Cataloguing in Publication Data.
A catalogue record for this book is available from the British Library.

ISBN 978 1 4456 5998 5 (print)
ISBN 978 1 4456 5999 2 (ebook)

Typesetting and Origination by Amberley Publishing.
Printed in Great Britain.

Contents

Foreword

This book has a tremendous amount of historical lore, cartographic accuracy, and original research, but it is one that could never have been written by a purely academic scholar.

Emma Brown is instead a hands-on, or rather 'waders-on', searcher after hidden underground truths, who has pursued her interest in the early development of Stockport to the extreme length of swimming in polluted rivers and crawling down death-trap tunnels to check the facts. On occasion she has come close to unconsciousness from hypothermia, braved poison gas in enclosed spaces and had rocks hurled at her by naughty boys. Sensible people may shake their heads, but fortunately I'm not very sensible and salute her instead. Excavating and crawling down cold, muddy, water-filled tunnels is one of the things that made Britain great, and requires a particular form of courage. It's also a great form of urban recreation.

The book is not wholly about water tunnels. Caves in Stockport's sandstone rock line the riverbanks, many of which may have been inhabited in prehistoric times, and some are still inhabited today. These are explored along with the air-raid tunnels of the Second World War – several complexes exist, in addition to the shelters open to the public in Chestergate. Railway tunnels are surveyed, including that linking the former Tiviot Dale Station under Lancashire Hill, remarkable for its interesting colours. Mills with their water tunnels and wheel pits are recorded, before indifferent owners and cash-strapped authority allow them to decay further.

I say don't try exploring the tunnels yourself, but instead read her book; go with Emma and her intrepid band of explorer friends in their rubber dinghy, on an intriguing cruise through subterranean Stockport.

Steve Cliffe, editor of *Stockport Heritage Magazine*

Preface

In 2005 I read a newspaper article about people who explored storm drains and sewers beneath their cities, photographing and documenting their experiences. To me this seemed like an exciting thing to do, an adventure into a subterranean world on your own doorstep. I became involved with caving and urban exploration groups and discovered that Stockport has a wide range of underground places, including a large number of water tunnels.

I thought I knew Stockport but actually all I knew were the everyday places, the high-traffic routes through town that we take for granted: Wellington Road, Merseyway shops, and landmark buildings like the Town Hall, the Plaza, and Regent House. Then I started walking around the back streets photographing buildings and began to notice the variety of styles, intricacy and beauty of Stockport's older architecture. I caught glimpses of (what I would later find to be) three rivers – behind Chestergate tavern, underneath Asda and alongside Meadow Mill.

I spent many hours at Stockport Heritage Centre, in St Mary's Church, where I found a treasure trove of maps, books and photographs, and listened to fascinating stories from the lovely volunteers – all Stockport residents with a passion for local history and memories of a different town. Gradually I came to really know Stockport: when I look at a street or building I see the layers of history, the people and buildings that have inhabited that place from when it was farmland with fields and streams, through the factories of the Industrial Revolution, to the modern town of today. Look up at St Peter's buildings, the art deco on Prince's Street, the Victorian marketplace – there's a story behind every façade. Look underneath the streets and you will find another forgotten world – subterranean Stockport.

My initial interest was in water tunnels, which were used to supply corn, silk and cotton mills from the seventeenth to eighteenth centuries. From the Goyt and Tame in the east to the Mersey in the west, Stockport's riverbanks are dotted with mysterious holes. I decided to investigate and photograph them all, little realising what I had let myself in for. Firstly, there were far more holes on the riverbanks than I had imagined, many of which would be challenging to reach. Secondly, going underground is much more risky than exploring above ground. There were dangers that had to be assessed and overcome.

In the pursuit of water tunnels I also discovered old and new sewers, forgotten streams, inhabited caves and ancient rooms. Some of the tunnels already had names, from their purpose or the people who built them. Those that, as far as I know, have not been mapped or named have been given appropriate names from their origins or features.

When we set out I knew a bit about local history, and had some caving experience, but brought more enthusiasm than practical skills to this project. It would not have been possible without the expertise of my exploring companions, Dan and Lee, in areas including but not limited to sailing, map-reading, algebra, surveying, sandwich-making, woodwork, and stick-poking. The book contains what we have investigated so far, but it is by no means a full account of subterranean Stockport. The adventure continues...

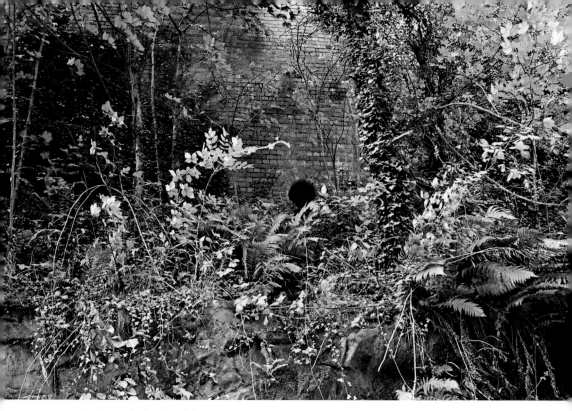

Drain on the banks of the River Mersey.

Introduction

On summer days we ventured into secret places along Stockport's riverbanks, and sat listening to the constant chatter of birds and insects hiding in the undergrowth. Bright blue dragonflies sparkled as they buzzed past, sand martins chirruped as they swooped low over the river to catch flies. I pushed my fingers into warm, soft sand. Under a clear blue sky and lush green leaves it felt like being on a remote beach, far from civilisation. I wondered how we had beaches so far inland.

The answer lies in the geology of this area. Stockport sits on a sandstone outcrop in the Cheshire Basin, an expanse of sedimentary rock which used to be seabed, laid down around 250 million years ago, which extends from Manchester to Shropshire. The basin was formed by slow-flowing glaciers depositing minerals such as calcium carbonate (from the shells of marine animals) and silicon dioxide (quartz). These particles were pressed into the colourful layers of rock you can see today – the red colour comes from iron ore. Rain and rivers have eroded the sandstone, and sand has been deposited on the riverbanks.

People have lived in the Stockport area for tens of thousands of years. The combination of a high vantage point, varied woodland, flat land suitable for agriculture, and a plentiful water supply made the area ideal for settlement. These conditions were also ideal for industry: a damp climate, needed for cotton spinning (to keep the threads moist) and a local supply of water and coal, to power the machinery. Waste water discharged from mills was hot. Fish, including goldfish and carp, flourished. A nineteenth-century dye-works owner claimed 'fish came about his works rather than other parts of the river, and the state of obesity which those fish attained was something striking'. Exotic plants grew on Stockport's riverbanks, from seeds brought in from Egypt with the raw cotton, and botanists flocked to see them.

Archaeological digs, such as those at Bridgefield and Edward Street (*see* 'Windmills', p. 36), and construction work have uncovered evidence of past occupation – including Bronze Age urns at Portwood and Roman coins at Heaton Lane – and no doubt will continue to do so. There are plenty of unexplored parts of town that could hold ancient artefacts.

Water Supply

Stockport's drinking water initially came from its many springs and wells. In 1795 the old town was supplied with water from springs in Barn Fields (near the town hall) and flowed into a reservoir behind St Peter's Church. From there it was piped to houses around the marketplace and to the market fountain. In 1817 a spring in Shaw Heath was described as 'a chalybeate spring of some strength'. It had a reputation for healing sore eyes. Early in the seventeenth century, chalybeate (iron-rich) water was believed to have health-giving properties. Anaemia caused by iron deficiency was not widely recognised at that time, though it was probably fairly common among those with a poor diet. Regularly drinking chalybeate spring water would have had a noticeably beneficial effect on health. Water from Barn Fields later fed a reservoir at Spring Bank Mill, which stood in the Grand Central area near the railway station.

In Heaton Norris there was a 'magnificent spring of pure cold water that issued from the red sandstone rock which the occupants of Hope Hill and Heaton Lane patronised very much'. Water from springs at the head of Hempshaw Brook, in Woodsmoor, was carried in cans on carts for distribution. Lord Street, near the library, had several springs with water 'running out at wooden spouts, from which women carried home their daily supplies in brown pitchers'. At the bottom of Pickford's and Bearhole Brows (opposite Adlington Square) the schoolhouse pump was a popular source of water.

From the 1820s Peter Marsland supplied water, drawn from springs in Woodbank Park, and the River Goyt, to public standpipes and later, private houses. By the 1850s his son Henry Marsland, leading the newly formed Stockport Waterworks Co., pumped water from a 45-metre-deep artesian well in the park (the area of the town centre where Sainsburys now stands) to a reservoir in Woodbank Park. An artesian well taps into an underground layer of water, which is under pressure and rises by itself without pumping, until hydrostatic equilibrium is achieved – the principle behind siphoning (see 'The Newbridge Cut', p. 47). There were two reservoirs for this drinking water in Woodbank Park: first it went into a mud-lined reservoir, from which sludge was dug out when it settled, and piled up around the sides. Then the water went to a sett-lined reservoir. It was alkaline so, to reduce the amount of lime in the water, Marsland ran it through filter beds before distribution.

Old maps of Stockport are liberally dotted with wells. One well, under Castle Yard, is believed to date from around 1150. There are also wells under the old Spread Eagle inn on Lower Hillgate; under Robinson's Brewery in Millgate, which 'supplied a trough with water for the use of beasts of burden'; and in Woodbank Park near Vernon Park Museum.

In 2014 United Utilities uncovered what was thought to be an old well underneath Wellington Mill (the Hat Works museum) on Daw Bank. We heard about this and couldn't resist taking a look. The hole was covered with a loose board and the area fenced off for safety. On our first visit we moved the board aside and saw a low brick arch above a huge shaft. It was over a metre in diameter, a neat cylinder carved out of sandstone. Torchlight revealed dark water of unknown depth, a couple of metres below the surface. We dropped a rock and heard it plunge into the deep.

We revisited a few days later with a camera, and a plumb line. This time the water level had gone down. My torch reflection was a tiny twinkle in a distant puddle. I lowered the line and it stopped around 5 metres down. We don't know for sure, but guessed that the water had been pumped out, rather than drained from the bottom.

When Wellington Mill was used for spinning, it had a beam engine to the south with a horizontal driveshaft which ran along the west wall on the first floor. This turned a vertical driveshaft at the south west of the building. The opening for the upright shaft was described as having 'a surround of massive sandstone blocks, the inner face of which had been dressed to accommodate a bevel gear wheel of c 2m diameter'. This 'well' is at the north-west corner of the building – could it be a second vertical driveshaft?

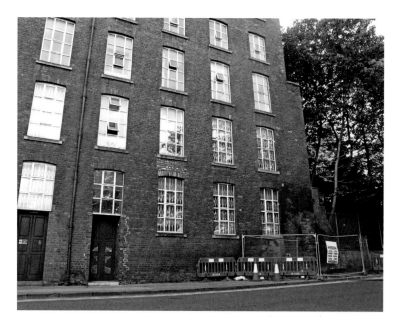

Wellington Mill.

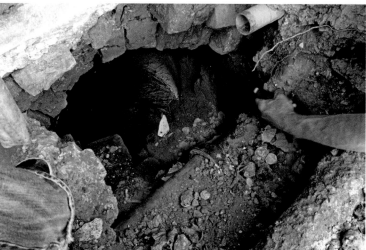

Wellington Mill shaft.

Cellars

In the last few years building work has uncovered several buried cellars. Archaeologists working at Bridgefield found lots of objects including toilets, chamber pots, shoes, bottles, and toys. Some of the finds will be displayed in the new Redrock development; others have been donated to Stockport Heritage Trust.

Nos 7–9 Lower Hillgate

The plot of land at the corner of Lower Hillgate and Rostron Brow was once owned by Rector Charles Prescot. In 1873 he leased to Thomas Kay, chemist and druggist, 'buildings, vaults, warehouses etc., built thereon, for 99 years at a yearly rent of £15'. In 1887 the lease was transferred to John Cash Arnfield, also a chemist, who ran the shop at Nos 7–9 Lower Hillgate and later a laboratory behind the shop in Harvey Street. By 1922 the buildings fronting Lower Hillgate had become a bank. In the 1980s there was an Italian restaurant here. The site was derelict for some years, until the construction of

Old cellar at Nos 7–9 Lower Hillgate.

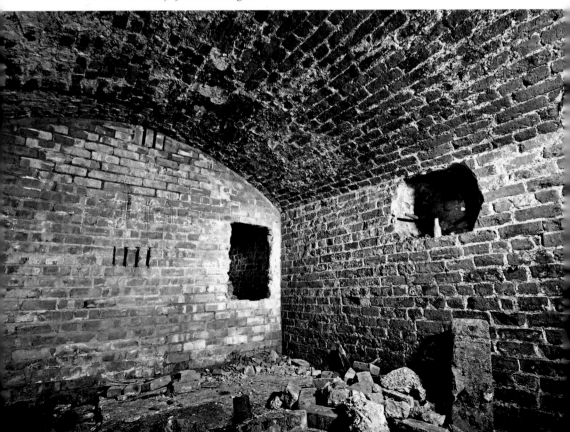

new flats in 2010. Demolition revealed a curved brick wall (maybe a chimney base), the roof of Tin Brook culvert snaking across the site and a couple of underground rooms, including the one in the photograph.

Wellington Street/Lower Hillgate

The area at the corner of Wellington Street and Lower Hillgate contained the Liberal Reform Club (later Peaches nightclub), Bishop Brown Industrial School, Church and Boys' Home and the Nonconformist Graveyard. Until the Education Act of 1902, children's education was conducted by religious organisations. The school was under the management of Sister Angela and seven sisters of the Order of the Immaculate Conception. It closed in April 1924. Since then the buildings were used as workshops, a DIY shop, and a martial arts centre. The graveyard had an archaeological investigation, revealing gravestones at different levels as well as many empty vaults. It is thought that the bodies were relocated when the graveyard went out of use. Another find was a possible medieval pit, showing habitation early on in this area.

The site previously contained Swain's Mill and R & W Brownsword, Ironmongers. I heard that builders found a tunnel, perhaps from Swain's Mill, which led some way and contained a steam engine. I didn't get the chance to confirm this, and the land has now been built over by the new extension to the boys' home. The other buildings have been restored and converted to flats, preserving the attractive façade. The photograph shows a small cellar which was underneath the Reform Club, facing Lower Hillgate. It had a brick fireplace and a stone shelf.

Old cellar under the Reform Club.

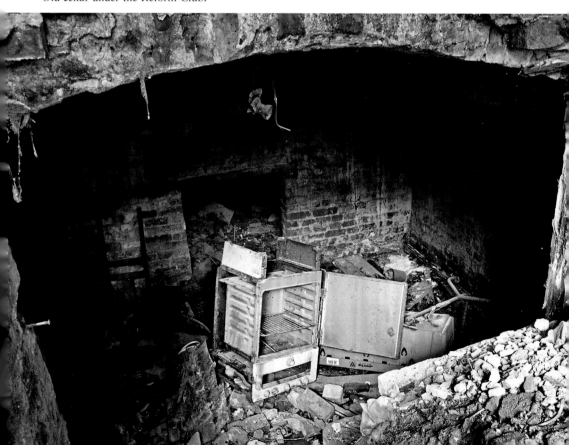

Mealhouse Brow

When building work commenced at Mealhouse Brow in the 1990s, several cellars and rock chambers were discovered. Stockport Dungeon, at the top of the Brow, has two 'cells' carved out of the bedrock, one of which can be seen through the small window on the hill. They were used for temporary holding of prisoners. Farther down the hill, inside a shop, I was shown another chamber. The proprietor moved aside a clothes rail to reveal a small door at ground level. I crawled through it into a short passage which led to the tiny room shown in the image. It looks like a storage space, perhaps to keep food cool.

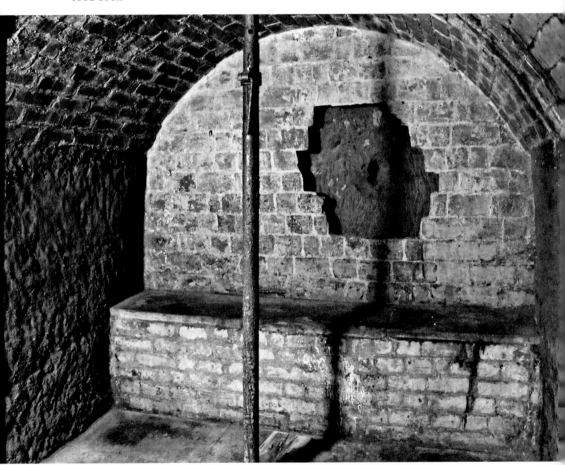

Old cellar under Mealhouse Brow.

Icehouses

Before electric refrigeration, the best place to keep things cold was underground. Pub owners, food retailers, and even homeowners in Stockport dug cellars into the sandstone bedrock. Those who could afford it imported ice from Scandinavia and others took ice from ponds in winter. A large block, properly stored (packed in sawdust or straw and kept underground), would last for months. Icehouses were built at George Warren's house in Poynton, Highfield House in Bredbury, the Old Rectory on Churchgate, and (possibly) Woodbank Hall. The last two are quite different in size and design.

The Old Rectory

There has been a building on the Old Rectory site since at least the fifteenth century. The present rectory was built in 1743 by the rector Ralph Stead. In the early nineteenth century, the rector was Charles Prescot. An icehouse thought to have been built during his time lies in its grounds. The icehouse was uncovered during an archaeological dig by Greater Manchester Archaeological Unit (GMAU) in 1991. It comprises two rooms: a rectangular outer room, and cylindrical inner room with a drain in the floor. The brick-vaulted roof is covered by a layer of clay which waterproofs and insulates it.

By 2015 the icehouse was neglected and full of rubbish. With permission from the Old Rectory manager, Stockport Heritage Trust members began clearing out the building and restoring it for people to visit. The icehouse now features on the 'black plaque' Town Centre Heritage Trail. It was officially opened by Dr Peter Arrowsmith of GMAU in March 2016.

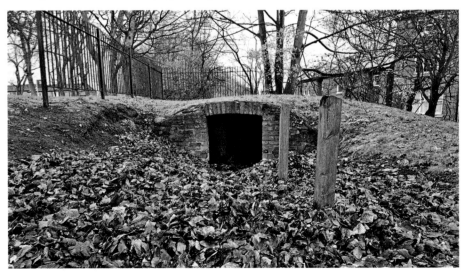

Old Rectory icehouse.

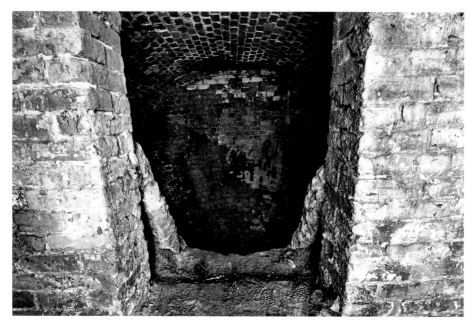

Storage chamber inside Old Rectory icehouse.

Woodbank Hall

The grand Woodbank Hall was the home of Peter Marsland and his family from 1814 and it was designed by the prominent architect and engineer Thomas Harrison, in a Greek style. The hall is a listed building and currently unused. The Friends of Woodbank Park group is working to enable the hall to be opened again for public use.

One day, Stockport Heritage Trust members were asked to help solve a mystery and as it involved going underground, I was invited along (or maybe I invited myself). At the back of the hall, part way down the steep bank towards the River Goyt, was a half-buried gate, behind which lay a brick tunnel – where did it go?

Once a considerable amount of soil had been dug out, the gate could be opened and I crawled inside. An old, cracked sewer pipe ran down the middle, possibly from the disused public toilets on the hilltop above. The tunnel opened into a large room that measured around 2 by 6 metres, and was nearly 2 metres tall with a deep layer of sludge on the ground. It had an arched ceiling with a neat oval opening at the back, covered from the top by a cream-coloured flagstone. Several more ceramic drainage pipes ran down the north wall. Although it was used for drainage, this room seems too big to have been built just to carry pipes. They look like later additions as the brick walls have been broken to fit them. Could it be related to the drain on the river known as the Ice House Sluice (*see* 'Marsland's Tunnels', p. 56)?

The Ice House Sluice doesn't appear to be close enough to drain from this building and is known to be a water tunnel, yet its name is the only clue we had to what this room might be. The design is not the typical conical shape of other icehouses and it is much bigger than the rectory icehouse. It could be a game larder for hanging meat to mature, although, again, it is not typical of those buildings which were usually above ground. Most likely it was a cold store, so perhaps there is a dedicated icehouse waiting to be found nearby.

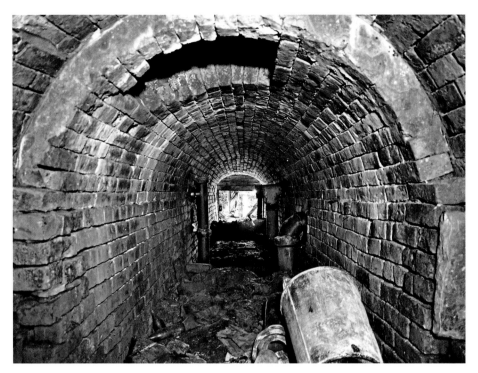

Woodbank Hall entrance tunnel.

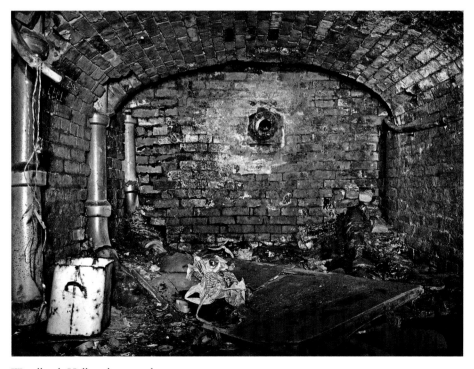

Woodbank Hall underground room.

Rivers

Stockport flourished because of its location at the confluence of the Tame, Goyt and Mersey. These three rivers (and their many tributaries) powered corn mills and, later, silk and cotton mills. They were instrumental in Stockport's industrial revolution, and the formation of the town we know today. Over the past three centuries Stockport's rivers have shaped progress, and been shaped by us. They have served as power sources, fishing spots, rubbish dumps, and sewers. We have carved and widened their banks in some places, and constricted them between stone and concrete walls in others. Gradually, as industry died out the rivers became natural havens again – fresh, clean and filled with wildlife.

I spent many enjoyable weekends down on the riverbanks, savouring these oases of calm under the bustling town. I rested under ferns clinging to damp, sandy outcrops, listening to the hypnotising sound of water gurgling over pebbles, bottles and bricks. Schools of tiny fish darted in the shallows. The rivers in summer have a unique smell: a combination of rich scents – sweet wild garlic, sour Himalayan balsam, pungent fox urine, heady hawthorn blossom, the ever-present undertone of sewage, and hints of past oil and chemical industries. I was amazed by the variety of animals – a cormorant lurking under a bridge, dippers bobbing among the rapids, wrens flitting through the undergrowth, rats hopping nimbly through riverside driftwood, and bats chasing flies on hot summer evenings.

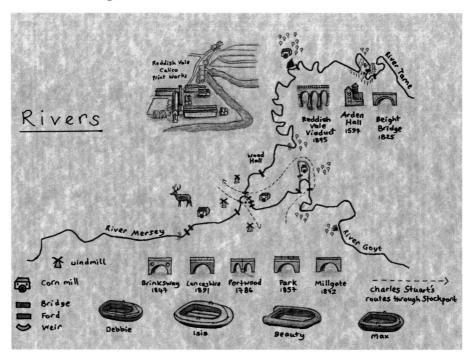

The River Tame

The gentle Tame originates in Denshaw Moor in the Pennines. Downstream, after Mossley, it becomes the traditional boundary between Lancashire and Cheshire. It flows towards Stockport through Delph, Uppermill, Stalybridge, Dukinfield, Haughton Green, and Reddish Vale. Its soft, sandy banks allow for it to spread outwards (as opposed to the Goyt and Mersey which are confined by sandstone and concrete walls, and rise upwards), which has resulted in erosion of its outer edges, forming many meanders, especially noticeable in Reddish Vale.

Denton waterworks is a partly active, but mostly derelict, water-treatment plant under Castle Hill in Bredbury. It sits between the curves of the Tame, in two sections connected by a light bridge. The buildings are crumbling and slowly disappearing beneath trees and ivy. The old pools used to filter waste water and discharged into the Tame. Nowadays the water in them is relatively clean; we found it filled with frogs and insects. After exploring the abandoned buildings, we took a dinghy and a picnic to the island.

One warm evening we entered the Tame underneath Beight Bridge: Dan and I in our second boat *Isis*, a chunky, sky-blue workhorse with a permanent slow puncture; Lee and Matt in *Beauty*, their tough, unsinkable inflatable. A wooden bridge 'just wide enough for a packhorse' was built here early in the seventeenth century. It has also been recorded as Bight, and Beet Bridge – Bight, meaning curve in the river, is probably the correct spelling. Round the first bend, to our right, smelly water gushed out of a small pipe – presumably overflow from the active part of the works. To our left sat the disused part of the works on a peninsula just 100 metres wide.

Next there was a long, straight stretch which flows through low farmland and under the high bridge carrying the M60. The river was warm and sluggish and we had to paddle hard just to keep moving forward. It was tempting to drift and enjoy the peaceful journey but we wanted to reach Stockport before dark and the Tame was in no hurry to get us there. We entered the flat-bottomed valley of Reddish Vale Country Park and caught sight of the viaduct, and to the right, the remains of an ancient millrace which runs parallel to the river for around 400 metres. Hazy, citrus sunlight shone low between the viaduct's spindly pillars.

Reddish Vale had a water-powered corn mill from the twelfth century, located near the confluence of the Tame and Denton Brook. In 1810 the mill was converted to a school and became known as the Ark because the brook could be seen flowing under the floorboards.

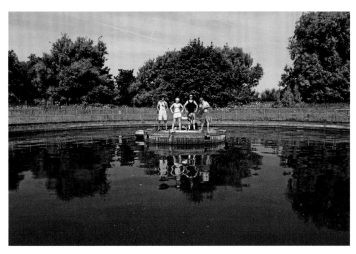

Denton Island.

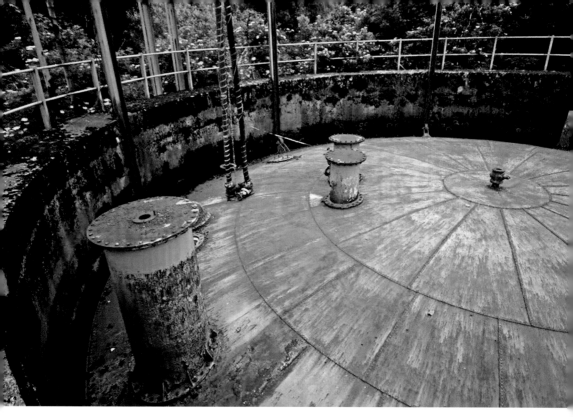

Above: Denton waterworks.

Below: Wet Welly Tunnel.

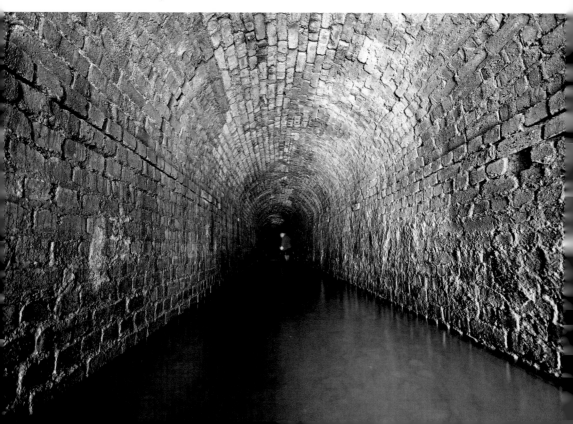

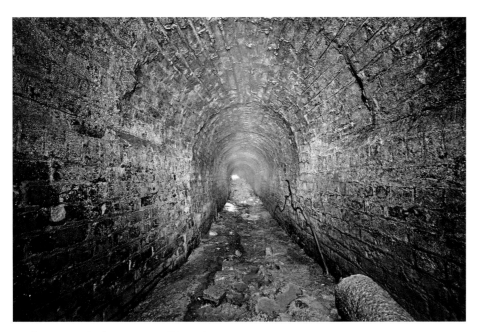

Looking towards the entrance of Tunnel One.

The Ark was later demolished to make room for two new reservoirs for the printworks. A printworks was first built in the Vale in 1780; it changed hands several times, expanded, and continued to operate as a print and dye works until 1952.

Denton Brook is one of around twenty small streams that contribute to the Tame between Beight Bridge and the Mersey. It is noticeably polluted, appearing grey and frothy. In 1875 the Ashburys to Romiley railway line was built over it, encasing around 40 metres of the brook in a nice brick culvert. Wet Welly Tunnel earned its name from the water being just deep enough to breech the intrepid explorer's welly.

Where there's a mill and water, there's usually a tunnel or two. Back in 2012, hidden behind silted banks and heavy undergrowth, Dan and Bill found a likely hole, later named Tunnel One. It wasn't very big, but the size of the arch suggested it would be if it wasn't filled with silt. I shone my torch in and saw a low space between the muddy floor and brick ceiling, but it looked like it might open up further in. Spiders' webs and moist slugs lined the surface of the roof. I put on a helmet, braced myself, and dived in. There wasn't enough space to kneel up so I lay down and dragged myself along with my elbows, pressing my feet against the walls and pushing my bag in front of me. I tried to think about anything but slugs and spiders. The floor dropped away and I rolled down into sloppy mud. I managed to stand up and found myself in a neat brick tunnel that had a row of yellow bricks between the upright walls and the arch, and was probably built by the 'cut and cover' method as it's not too far from the surface. I scampered over soft, orange sludge to the end, some 15 metres away where a rusty metal plate held back rubble. The arch ended and the wall straightened. It looked like this could have been the location of a sluice gate and the beginning of an open channel.

The first time we explored Tunnel Two, I wasn't prepared for how difficult it would be. There was a gap between mud and brick, and it was even smaller than Tunnel One. I volunteered to investigate, and Dan and Bill agreed that it was far too small for them. I suspect they meant it was too filthy for them or, to use a caving term, 'squalid'. Water flowed out over smelly black mud, and thick roots penetrated the brick roof, making it

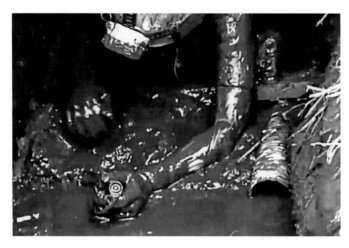

Emerging from Tunnel Two.

difficult to go beyond the first couple of metres. I slid in, flat out, unable to lift my head to look in front of me; I couldn't push my helmet past a bump in the mud. My helmet is 8 inches wide, which is the smallest gap I can squeeze through, so if the helmet doesn't fit, I won't fit. Blindly, I scraped at the mud with my fingers but couldn't reduce the gap. My breath filled the tiny air space with steam. I decided to give up for now and slid back out.

I was only wearing a fleece caving suit and it was wet and filthy so I sat in the Tame to wash myself down. The water was bracing and I gasped as the cold hit my back – it must have been meltwater from the snowy hills – and I went to find a sheltered spot to get changed. I was shivering as I tried to remove my boots. Time, and my mind, seemed to slow down. I was colder than I'd ever been before. I stared at my laces but couldn't remember how to take boots off. I struggled half-heartedly with my sleeves before giving up. Time stopped and I was stuck in this dreamy moment – wet and cold, but inexplicably content. Fortunately my companions checked on me and realised I was hypothermic. They encouraged me to change, took off my boots, and wrapped me in a thick coat. They made me walk around, then gave me tea and biscuits and waited patiently until I stopped shaking and regained my faculties. Had I been alone the outcome could have been much worse.

The second time I went into Tunnel Two I was better prepared: wetsuit, neoprene gloves and a saw. I scrabbled into the black hole. I was determined there wouldn't be a third visit to Tunnel Two, so hacked vigorously at the roots and mudbank until I could move on. Only a few metres farther and I reached the end. Although I couldn't kneel up, it was just wide enough that I could curl up on my side and spin around to face the exit. A plastic pipe poked through a hole in the bricks, pouring cold water into the tunnel which must have been surface drainage. I grabbed an old brick to show Dan and Bill – mission accomplished. I wriggled as fast as I could towards the light and slithered out of Tunnel Two.

Back to the boat trip: *Isis* and *Beauty* bobbed past the entrances to tunnels One and Two. As far as we know, they are the only remains of the printworks' tunnels. The area is now a park and nature reserve. The final stretch of the Tame winds tortuously through the valley, surrounded by a golf course and farmland – not as dramatic as the Goyt and Mersey gorges, but pleasant and open. The river flows fastest on the outside bends which, if they're shallow, make for a choppy ride. However, we had to protect our inflatables from the riverbed, and vice versa. We paddled into deeper water where possible, leaning low over the prow and ducking to avoid being disembarked by overhanging willows. We kept an eye and ear out for our landing point – anywhere we could haul the boats out before we were swept over Harrison's (Portwood) Weir. The weir is the largest in Stockport, around 5 metres high. Although some of its steps have fallen into the river, the sloping design can still be seen.

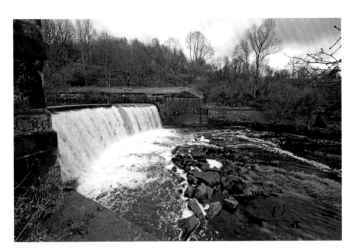

Harrison's Weir.

We might not have survived going over it, but the roar of the falls could be heard in plenty of time so we scrambled onto the bank and ported the boats beyond the weir.

Portwood Cut and Harrison's Tunnel

A short diversion of the Tame was cut (across the bend behind Meadow Mill) before 1700 and supplied water to corn mills in Portwood which, by the late eighteenth century, belonged to James Harrison of Manchester, who also owned the manor of Brinnington. As Harrison's business expanded to cotton spinning, he needed more water power and decided to build another diversion. An 1820 map shows a footbridge over the River Tame below Wood Hall in Reddish, and a ford a little further upstream. At that time the river had a bend there which would seem a convenient point from which to take water, however when Harrison built his weir in 1796 he chose a site much farther upstream. Although it meant digging a longer channel, the river above the weir was at a higher elevation than Portwood and had a natural fall. The first section of the channel ran through a tunnel in the sloping bank, opening out once it reached lower ground. This bank was known as Waterfall Bong. The channel became known as the Portwood (or Porky) Cut. It was also called the Bottle Canal (1833) and later just the Bottle. The top of the tunnel entrance can just be seen above the weir and is almost fully submerged.

In the 1970s the Tame was straightened and the land levelled, so the Wood Hall bend no longer exists. The river was moved south-east and now flows towards Meadow Mill in part of the channel of the disused Portwood Cut. The bridge and ford would have been some distance to the west in Wood Hall fields and may still be buried there among the rubbish of the old Grimesbottom tip.

Once abandoned, Harrison's structures made for exciting playgrounds: they were popular for ice-skating in winter and swimming in summer. I was told this story by Harry Pendlebury, who lived in Portwood as a boy. In the 1940s he and his brother used to swim in the weir pool. Harry's brother and his friends would also jump off the weir, but Harry was scared and just climbed up the weir steps to watch them. When he was four years old he had fallen into the Porky Cut, downstream by the mills. Unable to get out, he started to sink below the surface. Fortunately his siblings' cries drew the attention of a local farmer, Mr Woodhouse, who ran over and pulled the boy out, saving his life. He carried him home on his cart and delivered the dripping bundle to his father, saying 'Is this yours?' Harry said he still remembers looking helplessly up through the murky water. Sadly, Mr Woodhouse himself met an early end. After a night out, he was travelling by train back home to Stockport which had to wait just before it reached Tiviot Dale station on the viaduct high above Portwood. It was dark and foggy outside. Assuming he had reached his destination, Mr Woodhouse got off the train and fell from the viaduct into a mill yard below. He was found in the morning, badly injured, and died soon after. When I exclaimed 'You have his life!' Harry just nodded.

We finally docked under Tiviot Way Bridge as the evening light was fading. A distance by road of just 2.5 miles took us nearly three hours. Assuming a top cruising speed of 3 miles per hour, and allowing for portage around the weir, we had sailed around 6 miles of river.

The River Goyt

The tempestuous Goyt and its tributaries the Etherow, Sett, and Black Brook contribute considerably more water to the Mersey. The Tame drains an area of 146 square kilometres; the Goyt, 365 square kilometres. It rises on Axe Edge Moor near Buxton. The name Goyt is thought to come from Middle English *goit* – a channel carrying water, or Old English *geotan* – flow. Until the nineteenth century Stockport was frequently flooded by huge volumes of water pouring down from the Peak District and spilling over the riverbanks. The old bridge on Newbridge Lane was taken away by flood in 1798. Two things helped alleviate the problem: the river gorge was deepened and widened, and in the twentieth century the Fernilee and Errwood reservoirs were built in the Goyt Valley, easing the impact of heavy rain. The rivers still rise by up to 3 metres, but only occasionally breach their banks.

Bakehouse graffiti.

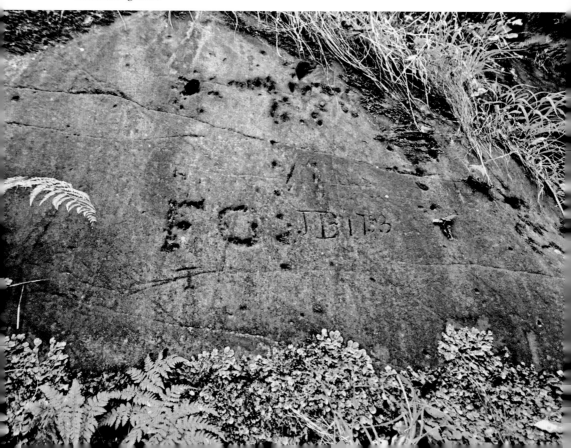

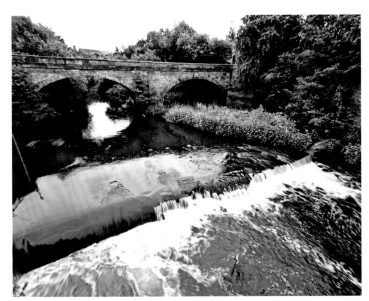

Portwood Bridge.

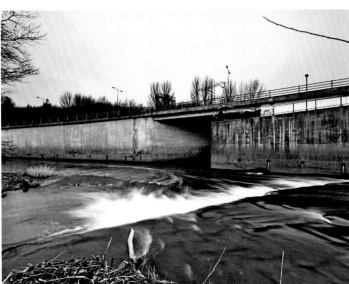

Confluence of the Tame and Goyt.

Widening the River

The men who worked on widening the river in the late eighteenth century lived in a 9 by 12 foot rock chamber cut into the north-east face of the hill in Vernon Park, at the site of the present rockery. The cave was later cut away and the sand used for 'foundry purposes'. The works extended from Bredbury Hall Bottom to Brinksway. We found a few examples of initials carved in rock at river level, not easily accessible from above. Could these have been made by the river workers? These carvings, near the exit of the Bakehouse tunnel, read 'FG' and 'JB 1793'. The lettering is neat and formal. Downstream, near Portwood Hall Cave, 'WW' is carved in what looks like a cleanly cut rock face.

Portwood Bridge

The oldest original bridge still standing in Stockport, Portwood Bridge, was built by James Harrison in 1786 to create access between his Portwood mills and Stockport town centre. There was an earlier bridge, shown on 1731 and 1777 maps, probably just a wooden packhorse bridge. The iron marker in the north parapet is a town boundary post.

The River Mersey

The River Mersey was the ancient divide between the Saxon kingdoms of Mercia and Northumbria, from where it gets its name. The Old English word *mearc* means boundary. Its source is high on Dark Peak above Glossop, though on some maps it was labelled as where the Etherow joins the Goyt. Today the river takes the name Mersey at Stockport and this point is marked by decorative railings on the footpath above the confluence of the Tame and Goyt. A recent, beautiful artwork on the wall over the confluence collages images of industrial Stockport. Historical accounts of the Mersey's source include, 'The Merseie riseth among the Peke his [Longendale], and from thence going downe to the Woodhouse [Woodhead] ... it méeteth with a faire brooke increased by sundrie waters called Goite,' (1535); 'we come next to Merpool [Marple], and there the Goit meets with the Merzey,' (1621); 'the River Mersey (or as some call it the Edrow) in the parish of Glossop,' (1772); and 'the Mersey is formed, and first receives its name, by the confluence (near Stockport) of the Thame and Goyt,' (1837).

Before the eighteenth century there were just three places to cross the Mersey in Stockport: two fords and one bridge.

Neale's Ford

An 1854 account of 'beating the bounds', a tradition of walking the town boundary, records this observation: 'The township ... terminates at, or about, a jutting point of rock which may be seen from the [Brinksway] bridge, and which was once known as Neale's Ford.' Hollywood Way Bridge now obscures this view but walking along the north bank you can follow the footpath as it drops close to river level, where the Mersey is wide and

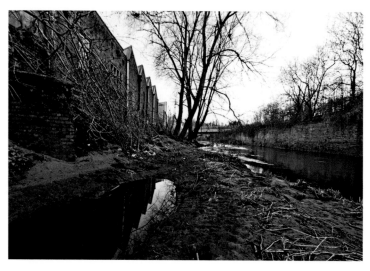

Neale's Ford.

relatively shallow. My photograph was taken near Heapriding Mill, which is on Ford Street. A crossing in this area is marked on 1731 and 1791 maps, although that may be Brinksway Bridge, which was rebuilt in 1847, but had previously been a narrow brick bridge. The ford could be much older than that.

Mersey Ford

Better documented is the Mersey Ford, having been used by the Romans and Prince Charles Edward Stuart. In the (now closed) Vernon Park Museum there was a paving stone taken from the Mersey at Stockport, thought to be from the ford. The Roman road from Manchester came down Dodge Hill towards the bottom of Lancashire Hill. The Romans paved all their roads, including fords. Mersey Ford is described as being 200 yards above Lancashire Bridge, and 60 yards below the confluence. In the winter of 1745, despite Lancashire Bridge having been destroyed and trenches cut in the ford in an attempt to thwart their progress, Prince Charles and his men waded across the Mersey at Stockport, en route to Derby. Around 120 men with horses and artillery also crossed at Cheadle, after recruiting local people to cut down poplar trees and build a bridge. Heginbotham offers this account of Charles' retreat: 'returning from Derby... along Turncroft Lane, down Royle's Lane [in Vernon Park], over the New Bridge, turning left they crossed the Tame, and so reached Manchester'. Perhaps the weather didn't favour a ford crossing – the king had lost a ship and all men in tempestuous weather a fortnight earlier. It was a cold, wet December – the rivers may well have been too high. The Jacobites certainly travelled back by several routes, including Cheadle, and reconvened before reaching Manchester.

Lancashire Bridge

There has been a bridge at the bottom of Bridge Street Brow since medieval times, though the current bridge is not the original one. There was an early reference to a bridge here in 1372, when a licence was granted by the Bishop of Lichfield to Thomas, a chaplain, to hold service in his hermitage, at the end of the bridge. Fords were often found near ancient churches, which were built by the side of rivers to enable passage across them, avoiding

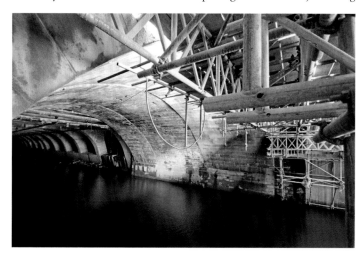

Lancashire Bridge.

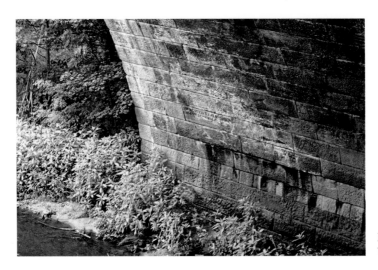

Date stone under
Wellington Bridge.

military or turnpike roads. There is evidence of the bridge being guarded in 1747, perhaps as a result of the Jacobites' visit. In that year a petition was submitted for expenses, for the constables on watch at the bridge, to prevent cattle crossing.

Flooding often caused damage to bridges and the areas surrounding Stockport's rivers. In 1615 it was noted, 'runs Merzey with great force, or rather fury, under a great stone bridge' and in 1662, 'upon the 30th January it was an extraordinary flood ... it filled the arch within about a foote'. The year 1799 saw a great storm devastate Stockport. The *Manchester Mercury* reported that many bridges and weirs on the Mersey, Tame, Medlock, and Irk had been washed away. The high water level was marked by a stone which is now set in the wall of Barclays Bank on Percy Street, to the left of the Buck and Dog entrance façade. It was originally on the steps that led from Warren Street down to a side entrance of the Buck and Dog, at a lower level than its current position. It reads, '17 August 1799 This River was as high as top of this Stone James Brown [the owner of the inn].' During a flood in 1866 the Mersey rose over 6 metres and the surrounding low land was covered in water. There are several stones marking that event: the east-facing wall under Asda's car park, visible from Park Bridge; the wall in the arch (a water tunnel exit) next to Portwood Bridge; the south-facing abutment of Wellington Bridge, visible from the Bearpit in Merseyway. They read, 'HEIGHT OF RIVER NOV 11th 1866 [REFIXED DEC 1892] or [REFIXED JAN 1893].' In the 1970s the Mersey flooded shops and cars on Chestergate, flowing up via Tin Brook at Adlington Square. A wall had to be knocked down near Ford Street to let the water back out into the river.

In 2015, part of Warren Street was removed to reveal Lancashire Bridge and you can now see the rebuilt central arch, with additions on either side from when it was widened in 1891.

Merseyway

The area between Mersey Bridge (under the road in front of Merseyway Shopping Centre) and Wellington Bridge is named the Bearpit, for the bear-baiting that once took place there. Bearhole Brow above Chestergate was named for a sandstone cave in which a bear was kept. Bear-baiting was prohibited in 1835, though a performing bear was reported in the town as late as 1887. The Bearpit was improved in the 1930s and work began to build a road over the River Mersey. In 2015 work was done to lighten the Bearpit by filling the steps with blocks of foam, as its weight was affecting the Merseyway arches beneath it.

I was told that workers found French writing on walls during the construction of Merseyway before concrete for the foundations was poured in; perhaps it was written by nineteenth-century prisoners of the Napoleonic War. In 1795 there were 13,666 prisoners of war in Britain and by 1798 this number had risen to 35,000 – the government desperately needed more prison space and advertised for suitable buildings. A total of 122,000 French and allied prisoners of war were held in Britain between 1803 and 1814. Some of these were held in Stockport. There was a late eighteenth-century prison, the 'County Lock-up', on Mill Lane (later Melville Street) which ran between the river and Warren Street from Lancashire Bridge. The prison was built directly over the riverbank, its small windows secured with thick bars. It was later repurposed as a mill, and finally demolished in 1985.

Dan, Lee, Matt and I decided to find out what was hidden under Merseyway, and, of course, get decent pictures. First, what kit should we take? I had taken photographs before, and seen other peoples' online; none of them captured the full scale of the structure. The concrete bridge is around 400 metres long. Light from outside doesn't penetrate very far – in the middle it is completely dark. We would need serious lighting. Lee suggested his car battery-powered floodlight, which would be heavy to carry, but hopefully worth it. We gathered our kit: safety gear – helmets, waterproof headlights and buoyancy vests; photography gear – cameras, tripods, hand torches and dry-bags; sailing gear – two boats, three pumps, repair patches, duct tape and mooring rope.

Second, how do we get down there? We could start in the Goyt, which involves a steep climb down by Portwood Bridge, then getting over or around the weir. Or, if the fence under Knightsbridge is broken (at a spot frequented by homeless people, and known as 'The Beach'), we could climb down the brick wall and trek through thick undergrowth. This would be hard work with two boats, four people, their rucksacks, and 20 kilograms of lighting equipment. Although furthest away, the easiest entry point into the Tame would be under Tiviot Way Bridge.

Merseyway looking west.

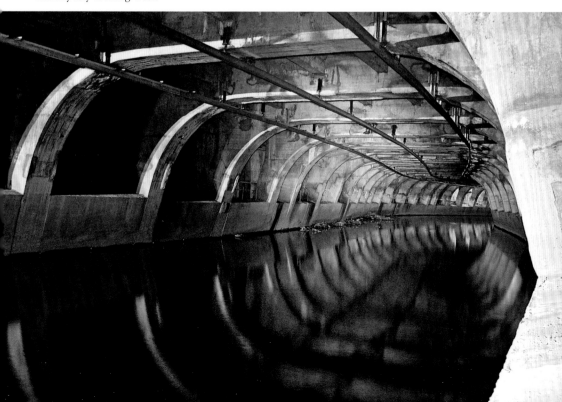

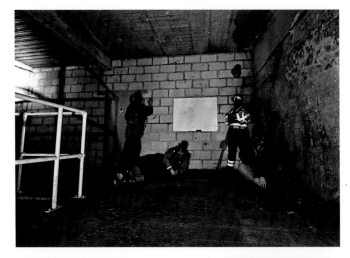

Gentlemen's toilets under Merseyway.

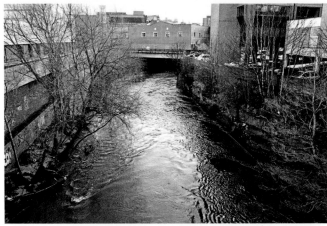

Entrance to Merseyway.

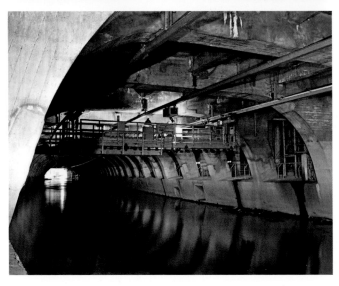

Merseyway looking east.

We laid out the boats and started inflating them. At this point in expeditions I always start to feel nervous and excited, my heart beating faster in Pavlovian response to the rhythmic wheezing of the pumps. We took turns with hand and foot pumps until our limbs ached, and *Isis* and *Beauty* sat swollen and sturdy in the sand. We pushed them into the water, waded out and jumped in. We drifted down the Tame, then plunged into the Mersey, accelerated by the rushing Goyt. Negotiating the obstacle course of dinghy-popping debris, we sailed into the darkness of Merseyway.

We headed for the north bank and found a pile of rubbish on which to jump out and moor our boats. The banks have concrete overhangs – not easy to access from the river should you fall in under here. We boosted and pulled each other up. In the nineteenth century large mills lined the banks of the Mersey. There are some remnants of buildings embedded in Merseyway, and of the underground toilets which used to be accessed from the precinct. I spoke to a man who helped build the substation down here. He said they found an old brick tunnel and when he shone his torch in it, hundreds of rats ran off into the darkness. Disappointingly, we couldn't find any sign of the tunnel. I often see rats around town in the early hours, foraging on quiet streets. Underground, tiny wet footprints in drains show they'd heard me coming just moments earlier and scattered. Bats also make their home under Merseyway, venturing out to hunt in the twilight.

A suspended, movable platform is used for Merseyway bridge inspection, which takes place every seven years – the last one was in 2010. It's a delicately balanced structure and we treated it gently. It was worth lugging the battery for this view – its golden beam illuminated the concrete arches spanning the black river. Their shimmering reflections gave the illusion of being in a giant wooden boat or a ribcage, like the belly of Jonah's whale. Once photos were taken and deemed satisfactory, we set sail again and landed downstream on a leeward shore.

Testing the Waters

As I often found myself submerged in local rivers, I wondered how clean they were. We took samples of water from various places and dropped them on agar in Petri dishes to see what grew. I put the dishes in my cupboard and checked after a couple of days. The Tame and Denton Brook (the blue dishes in the image) showed by far the most bacterial and fungal growth, with white and green colonies quickly filling the dishes. A few days later the Goyt and Mersey (the red dishes) had small colonies too. Our control plate (the yellow dish) only had one tiny patch of growth. The results were about what we expected from our different test sites: we suspected the Tame was much dirtier than the Goyt, and it is – another reason to avoid falling in.

River water samples.

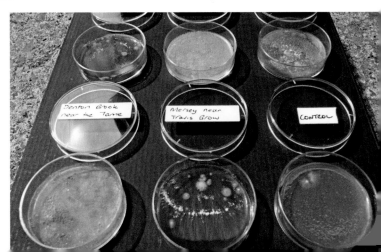

Caves

Having studied maps and books, walked the banks, and sailed all three rivers, we now had a long list of intriguing holes to investigate, the oldest of which were caves. A cave is an underground space formed by a natural process. Caves readily form in limestone due to the flow of water dissolving minerals and carving out passages. Sandstone caves are rarer. They are formed from gradual erosion by wind and water, usually on exposed cliffs and coastlines. As far as I know, Stockport has no natural caves. There are, however, several holes that have been named thus and this chapter looks at a few of those man-made 'caves'.

Devil's Cave

A pleasant stroll through Thatcher's Wood in Woodbank Park followed by a precipitous scramble along the Goyt's steep west bank lead to the entrance of what is known locally as the Devil's Cave. With no confirmed explanation of its origins, Dan and I decided to investigate and find out how old this cave really was.

The first thing we saw just before the entrance was a long, low stone shelf under overhanging rock – it makes for such a natural seating area that it could have been deliberately shaped for that purpose, perhaps to sit around a fire. The ground was warm and sandy. Delicate, long-legged spiders tiptoed over the colourful, weathered sandstone. The rock face was covered with visitors' calling cards – carved initials, names and dates.

Could this be an ancient cave? Neolithic tools have been found in Woodbank Park and it is possible people would have excavated a living space here. Neolithic people used antler picks to excavate and mine. It has also been suggested that this cave was part of the water-tunnel network built in the early nineteenth century. The cave is currently around 1.5 metres high, 2 metres wide and 4 metres deep. It has straight walls and an arched ceiling, patterned with crisp impact marks. Direct hits are triangular and sharp edged, more likely from a metal tool than a round-tipped antler.

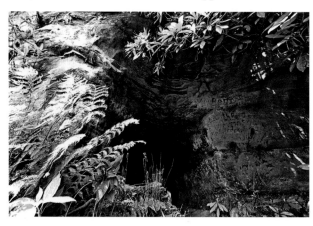

Devil's Cave entrance.

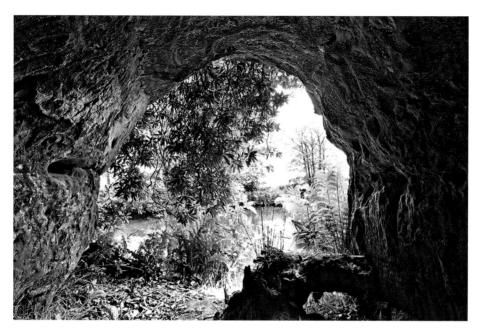

Looking out from Devil's Cave.

The floor is compacted soil and sand. We wanted to find out how deep it was so, armed with a shovel and a metre-long sharp stick, we started to dig. Around 1 metre down, through heavy brown mud, we hit a band of pale grey, sparkling mud that smelled chemical and familiar; it was the same smell as Hempshaw Brook just downstream of EC Pigments (*see* 'Hempshaw Brook', p. 74). We concluded that this layer was deposited during a time of industrial pollution at Glossop, possibly from Dinting Printworks. In 1864 the Stockport Waterworks Co. took Edmund Potter, head of the printworks, to court to resolve a dispute over water quality. Potter's works were polluting the river with arsenic, however the court found in his favour as the company only had the legal right to abstract water, not to regulate its quality. The Rivers Pollution Prevention Act (1876) should have ensured an end to this pollution. Below that was brown sand. One more shovel full and we hit water. We were now at river level, but not yet at the bottom of the cave. We pushed the stick deep into the hole; it slid down until just a hand hold was left above ground and hit solid rock. With Arthurian effort we pulled it triumphantly out of the sticky ground.

The cave's floor is around a metre below the current (summer) water level. The river was raised a little by the construction of the Nab weirs in 1819 and 1833 but even before then water might flow into here in all but the driest weather. We used the stick and found only solid walls at the back and sides. We may have disproved the Neolithic cave theory but the actual purpose of the Devil's Cave is still a mystery.

Newbridge Lane Cave

On a hot summer's day, when the river was low, I visited this cave with Magda and Paco. They were travelling and wanted to have an adventure so we packed my first dinghy – *Debbie*, a trusty, orange vessel of some years' experience, now more patches than boat – and headed into Stockport. We stopped on Newbridge Lane to tie an electron (lightweight caving) ladder to a tree above our cave. I checked it was secure then let it unravel and drop to the river. We walked around to Carrington Road footbridge and climbed over the railings. Grasping branches of the saplings on the steep bank, we swung down to the beach at the bottom. Barefoot, we stepped cautiously over warm sand and into the slippery, stony river. The water was shallow but cold and fast. Even on hot days this side of the river remains in the shade of north-east facing cliffs, keeping it cool, damp, and green. From the opposite side the cave looked dark and its depth uncertain. Paco grabbed the ladder, climbed up and along a ridge into the cave, then held out a hand to help Magda and I follow. From the outside it looks like a water tunnel exit (*see* 'The Ancient Corn Mill Tunnel', p. 36) with the tunnel at the river and a sluice above, however it is not marked on the CEGB survey of water tunnels.

We found ourselves in a space just 2 metres wide and 3 metres deep with a soft, sandy floor. Apart from a small section at the back, the walls were free of tool marks, smooth, and well worn. Lines between layers of sandstone were distinct. Perhaps it was excavated from the bottom up: miners chip at the bottom of an ore seam so it weakens and falls; I have seen Stockport tunnels with large flakes of sandstone fallen from the roof – the layers split apart easily. Was it excavated like that, or is it so old that the pick marks have weathered away? The walls had carved markings: lines but no distinct letters. They could be writing or maybe knife-sharpening marks – St Mary's Church in the marketplace has similar lines which are thought to be from the sharpening of arrow heads as archery was once practised in the churchyard.

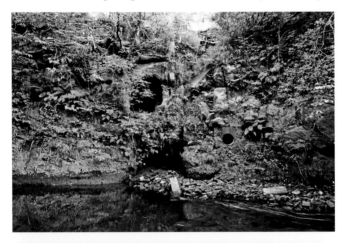

Newbridge Lane Cave from the riverbank.

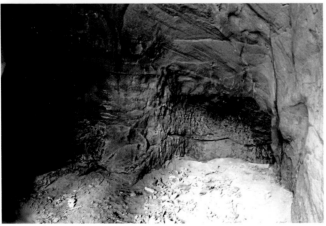

Inside Newbridge Lane Cave.

Mersey Caves

Known locally as Maggie's Caves, the various caves along the cliff at Brinksway have been inhabited and expanded over several hundred years. An early road from Stockport to Cheadle was cut through the rocks behind the caves. This road was widened and levelled in 1821 and made a picturesque scene 'like a gentleman's park, hung with vegetation and crowned with coloured masses on either side'. The date of the improvements was carved on a 'high ridge in the rock'. We looked for, but have been unable to find, this date. We did find some neat initials, carved in weathered sandstone, which can be seen along the footpath on the north side of Brinksway. A later account says this of Brinksway: 'it would take a brave man to walk the road at night, for the ghost of Peggy Travis who was foully murdered by drunken men, walks nightly, also the caves conceal assassins.'

Although it is known that some of the 'navvies' who worked on the construction of Stockport Viaduct from 1826 to 1840 lived in the Mersey Caves, they probably didn't excavate them. Possible candidates are the Ancient Corn Mill Tunnel diggers in the early eighteenth century, or the river wideners in the mid-eighteenth century, both of whom would have had the tools and experience to construct this large network. Houses existed here long before the viaduct was built.

An 1881 account says of the caves, 'hewn out of rock in the first instance, for the conveyance of a conduit of water – this was subsequently enlarged and used as a dye shop. In around 1851 it was used as a distillery for the purification of gas tar.' A small brick culvert emerges into the west side of the caves and drains into the river, sending a tiny waterfall splashing down the cliff. Its egg-like shape suggests it was a sewer at one time. It now drains rainwater or a small stream. A Mr Taylor occupied a house on the outcrop and worked the distillery; he used gas tar to produce naphtha, a fuel for burning. A pipe-maker also worked in a cave here. There is a narrow vertical shaft through the rock which may have been his, or Mr Turner's, chimney.

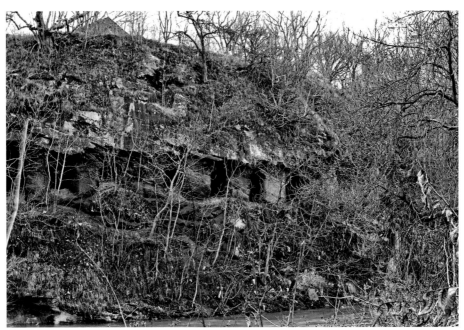

Mersey Caves from across the river.

A hollow, or cavern, cut out of the solid rock, eight yards long by four yards wide, light being admitted by two large apertures, forming a window and doorway. Attached to the house is another cavern about seven yards long and of irregular width, which is used as a kitchen, the back premises being on a ledge of rock high up from the sluggish river below.

The caves formed part of houses built into the rock face and stemple holes can still be seen where wooden beams were supported by the rock.

In 2009 I went to find what I knew as the 'Tramp's Cave', a dwelling close to, but not part of, the Mersey Caves. Apparently a man lived here for many years but had recently disappeared and was rumoured to have fallen into the river. I climbed over the wall by the road and crept carefully along a narrow trail, wary of slipping down the steep bank. There was a low hollow, not very wide, just a couple of metres deep. An excavated space, it may have been inhabited in the nineteenth century and appeared to be so now too. Inside was bedding, bags, and unopened food. I departed, leaving everything untouched.

A few years ago there was a story in the local press about an Eastern European man living in the Mersey Caves, who was subsequently rescued by his mother and, more recently, a local homeless woman fell from the caves and had to be rescued from the riverbank. On every visit to the caves I have found evidence of people living in these precarious places.

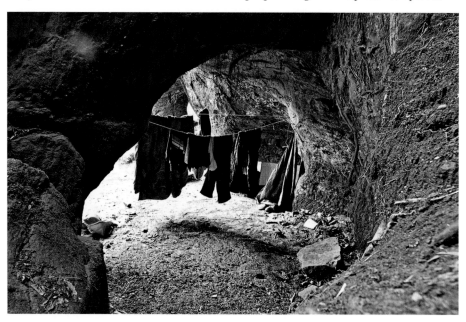

Inside Mersey Caves.

Water Tunnels

No other underground structures in Stockport are as big or impressive as the water tunnels, which were driven to provide a steady water supply to various mills. Although now disused, they remain a monument to the skill and hard work of the surveyors, engineers, and labourers who created them. The big three are the Ancient Corn Mill Tunnel, Stringer's Tunnel, and Marsland's 'Nine Foot' Tunnel, all of which take water from the River Goyt in Vernon and Woodbank Parks. I have also documented a few smaller tunnels that don't appear on maps.

Corn Mills

There are records of corn mills in Stockport from the thirteenth century, and it is likely they were in existence before then. They were powered by waterwheels built over brooks, rivers, or mill races (sluice gate controlled water, diverted from a natural source). They

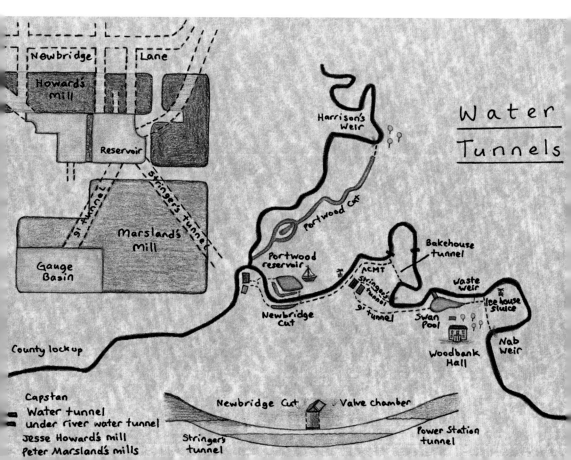

were owned by the Lord of the Manor, who compelled local farmers to grind their corn at his mill, taking a portion as his fee. By the eighteenth century corn mills were disappearing, with some being converted for silk and cotton spinning, which were more lucrative.

Windmills

Elevated ground on either side of the Mersey was the ideal location to capture the power of the wind sweeping along the valley from the west coast. There was a windmill on Edward Street (on the site of the recently demolished Hollingdrake's building) which was owned by William Robinson, who had a corn factory at the bottom of Hillgate. The miller was a one-armed man named Levi. It was a circular, conical building also used in the mid-nineteenth century to hold Chartist (campaigners for political reform) meetings. It was built in 1784 and demolished in 1857. There were also windmills on Wharf Street by Lancashire Hill, occupied by Thomas and James Heys, and on Hope Hill, near Travis Brow. However, wind power was erratic and stormy weather damaged sails on several occasions. Water provided a more reliable source of power and by the eighteenth century several entrepreneurial mill owners had already started excavating tunnels.

The Ancient Corn Mill Tunnel

A waterwheel at Millgate was carried away by a flood in 1644, with a new one being built to replace it. Further downstream, above Goyt weir and at the confluence, a waterwheel

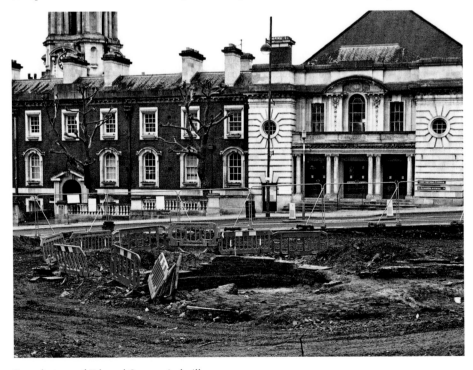

Foundations of Edward Street windmill.

was also washed away by floodwater, but never rebuilt. Regular flooding was costly to mill owners, in both repairs and lost earnings. As early as 1718 the Lord of the Manor, John Warren, began planning Stockport's first water tunnel, to supply his mills at Millgate and the Park. This mile-long tunnel would provide steady water flow and protect waterwheels from the river's extremes. It was an ambitious undertaking finally completed in 1743, by which time John and his brother and successor Edward had both died. Edward's son George became the new Lord of the Manor in 1737 at the age of two, and the executors of the estate completed the tunnel. The Ancient Corn Mill Tunnel (ACMT) runs from Vernon Park to the centre of Stockport.

The first section of the ACMT starts near the fountain in Vernon Park and exits under the junction of Newbridge Lane and Carrington Lane. This section became known as the 'Bakehouse Tunnel', presumably because it supplied corn mills that had their own bakehouses.

This was the one I wanted to see most of all. At nearly 300 years old, it is one of the earliest water tunnels in town. Its walls would have pick marks, and perhaps even graffiti, carved by pioneers. One warm summer's evening, Dan and I strolled through the beautiful Vernon Park, inhaling its intoxicating scents: lime and jasmine blossoms; the muskier tones of decaying leaves; and sweet, sticky resin dripping from damp tree trunks. We headed off the path to an unexplored corner. The location looked overgrown from above and we assumed any evidence of the tunnel had long since been buried. We gripped branches and creepers as we slid down the steep bank and came to a stop just above the river.

Although the tunnel entrance was blocked by a bank of soil and a well-established tree, above it, hidden behind a thick curtain of ivy, we found the sluice gate control. In the centre of this dusty, brick-arched room, a large iron wheel protruded from the soil. I wiped the cobwebs from its weathered surface. Dan pulled the wheel and for the first time in years it turned, then stopped. I was half hoping that something exciting would happen, but no secret passage opened up. Its exit is now sealed by what looks like bags of cement or sand. There is a brick wall on top which probably conceals a sluice control similar to the one at the entrance. In 1743 there were no bridges here: the bridge at Carrington Lane was built in 1864 and the current metal footbridge was built in the 1970s. Although there was later a group of buildings on the narrow piece of land above the Bakehouse Tunnel exit, they were not connected to it.

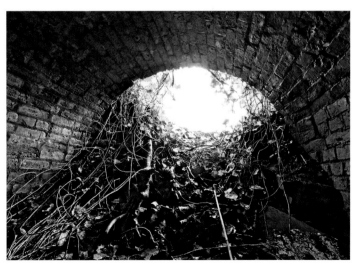

Bakehouse Tunnel sluice chamber.

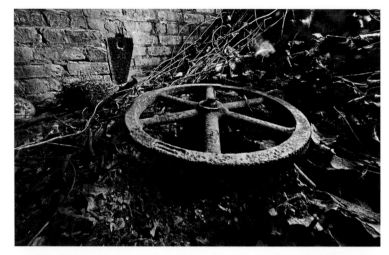

Bakehouse Tunnel valve wheel.

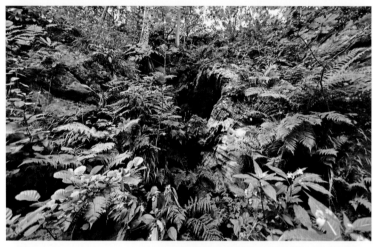

Jim Clare.

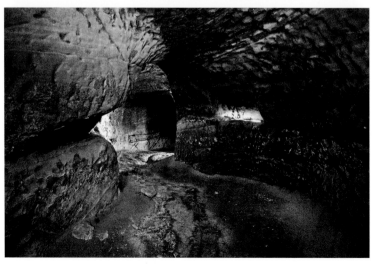

Inside Outcrop Tunnel.

Just before the Bakehouse Tunnel exit, the ACMT takes a left turn and follows the line of the Goyt towards Millgate. Along the way are several side tunnels into the river. We wondered why there were so many exits, they don't serve to feed any mills so maybe had something to do with its construction. Starting from different points on the riverbank would enable several sections to be driven at the same time. Another possibility is that they were for flushing out silt to prevent it from clogging waterwheels.

Jim Clare told me that in the 1950s he lived in a house on Newbridge Lane, and knew there to be a tunnel running right underneath it. It was one of the things that sparked his initial interest in the tunnels, which he passed on to me. For that reason, the first exit tunnel is named after him. The houses have since been demolished: all that remain are a few bricks and household objects in the river at the bottom of the cliff, and memories of old Newbridge Lane. A couple of metres up the cliff is a rock chamber filled with soft, dry sand. The water tunnel itself is probably at river level – we could only see mud and vegetation below the chamber.

The next tunnel is Star Street, where there was a rounded hole around 1.5 metres both in height and width, and just over 2 metres above river level. I climbed up the crumbling rock to find a concrete wall filling the hole. On the side wall were indentations, similar to those at Newbridge Lane Cave, which may have supported a wooden beam. One we didn't manage to locate lies beneath the pub and so is named Midway. It is hidden beneath a muddy bank and covered with heavy undergrowth. The next exit, east of Cromer, was inhabited. When we saw the bedding inside we decided not to go in. Like the others, there looks to be a river-level water tunnel that is blocked with silt and has a rock chamber above it. Heading downstream, the next few exits before St Mary's Way were adapted for Jesse Howard's and Peter Marsland's Newbridge Lane mills.

West of St Mary's Way and opposite Dunelm Mill, which occupies the site of the demolished Palmer Mills, is Outcrop Tunnel. It is situated high above the river so it seemed easier to access it from above. On this occasion I was accompanied by Zoe. It was a damp Sunday morning in March and the river was high. I attached an electron ladder and safety rope to the signpost on the path above the outcrop. We climbed over the new wall and down to a rock ledge. We then anchored the gear so it couldn't be pulled up from above. I went first along the narrow ledge. It was slippery with mud and leaves, and some 5 metres above the swollen river. Just in time, I turned back to check on Zoe and saw her lose her footing. She fell and started to slide down the cliff, but I managed to grab her wrist before she slipped out of reach. Thankfully she was light enough for me to pull up, or else we would both have gone for a swim.

This tunnel is a bit of a mystery. Its opening contains a bricked-up outlet from the ACMT. There is a slot in the roof which could have held a sluice gate. The rest of it, around 40 metres long and parallel to the river, seems superfluous. The tunnel starts tall and narrow, with walls that are more rippled by water than carved by hand. We could stand upright within it. It becomes wider around a dog-leg bend, and pick marks are visible. There is a shelf carved in one wall that was big enough to hold my torch, or perhaps a labourer's candle and pick. It then becomes smooth and rippled again and heads downwards, coming to a dead end, filled with sand almost to the roof. My feeling is that it must have been smoothed by water, therefore should open out on the other side of the outcrop. As yet, I haven't found an exit.

The next ACMT outlet is Corner Shop. Dan and I clambered and ducked along the narrow riverbank through brambles and knotweed, gathering leaves and cobwebs in our hair. Mossy walls rose out of the undergrowth like the ruins of an ancient temple. We noticed a trickle of water emerging from a landslide of mud which had fallen over a sandstone ridge. The water flowed clear and constant. We tested the pH and it was slightly alkaline, meaning either spring water or perhaps rainwater seeping through concrete. It may indicate that the ACMT is filled with water. With the Vernon Park entrance being sealed, it could come from cracks in the tunnel or drainage holes like those in Stringer's Tunnel.

In the nineteenth century, the ACMT emerged below the steps at Newbridge Lane and 'after an open flow the water entered two tunnels opposite to Millgate Hall [below St. Mary's Church]. The one to the right to supply the mill in Millgate, to the left leading to the mill near Lancashire Bridge. In the Corn Mill Sluice was a paddle [sluice gate], named before the Pleasure Walk Paddle'.

Until recently the footpath from Newbridge Lane to Millgate, which follows almost exactly the route of the ACMT, was overgrown with greenery: balsam, bamboo and blackthorn hid the path from view, and the view from the path. During the winter someone was living in a tent by the river, in what would be an idyllic spot in better circumstances. It is also the site of two shafts which we thought might lead into the ACMT. I will come back to them later (*see* 'The Newbridge Cut', p. 47). Then, in March 2015, the path and woodland were cleared and thinned. I miss the wildness, but have to admit it looks great. You can see the river, and all the way to St Mary's Church at the end of the winding path. It has become a 'pleasure walk' again.

Mooching about under Park Bridge, I noticed there were square holes at the bottom of both abutments. I thought perhaps the Portwood (east) side might be a tunnel from Peter Marsland's reservoir. There was too much debris in the river to get a boat close enough to moor, so I would have to wade. After a dry spell, the river was just low enough and I crept across, with water pushing hard against my legs. Jamming my feet against rocks and gripping rusty shopping trolleys, I eventually reached the other side. Disappointingly, it was filled to the top with mud. It was probably a drain of some sort, which explains why the gap was left when the bridge was built.

I wobbled back to the Stockport (west) side. This hole wasn't filled, but my torch wasn't bright enough to light up the end. I braced myself to crawl into the unknown – most of the time the holes are partly underwater and I didn't want to get stuck in there if the river started rising. Commando crawling as fast as I could, I came to a junction and was able to wriggle into a sitting position – legs folded up and arms pressed close to my sides. Above was a vertical shaft of blackened stones that stretched up to the street level. Ahead was the curved top of a narrow bricked-up sandstone tunnel; the rest of it would be below river level.

Park Chase Tunnel predates Park Bridge – workers built over it in 1857, which was possibly also when it was sealed. An 1850 tunnel map shows an inlet here but it is not linked to any branch of the ACMT. It could have supplied an earlier corn mill, and was

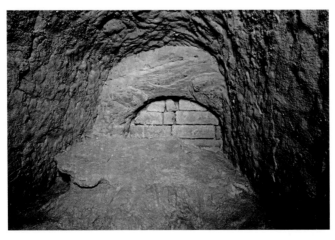

Bricked-up tunnel in Park Chase.

perhaps linked to the Mill Dam, a reservoir in the park that was used before the ACMT was excavated. It may be even older than the Bakehouse Tunnel.

Warren Street (later Faulder's) Mill next to Park Bridge was built around 1790. In 1871 it burnt down and was rebuilt. Faulder's Mill was demolished in 1989. The only remnant of the original building is its boiler house, which sits next to Park Bridge, hidden behind undergrowth and billboards. I think the shaft from Park Chase could have been a drain for this boiler house. Underneath the mill on the riverbank is Greenstone Tunnel, which is part of the ACMT network. Lauren and I started to dig it out, but it's very low and as soon as it rained the river washed silt back in and filled it up again.

Park Mills

The Park's position made it ideal for capturing water, and mills were built here as early as the thirteenth century. Park Mills, owned by Peter Marsland, covered most of the area where Sainsbury's is now. A network of tunnels brought water from the ACMT to several large wheel pits, which were filled in during the construction of the supermarket in the 1980s. A few years ago the arches of Park Mill outlets could still be seen from Percy Street, behind the Buck and Dog, but several floods in recent times have washed more sand and debris up against the old wall and they are now buried.

Stringer's Tunnel

This tunnel was photographed in 2007 by explorers Dodgerat, Havoc and Mendoza who named it 'Deep Silt – The Beast of Stockport'. Although not the longest tunnel in town (444 metres from the weir to Howard's Reservoir), it was reputed to be difficult to travel through and, having done that several times, I can confirm it lives up to its name.

Stringer's weir and tunnel, built in 1791, are named after John Stringer, who leased a mill from William Howard, on Newbridge Lane. The reservoir at Newbridge Lane was at first filled just by Stringer's Tunnel, and the water shared with the neighbouring mill, owned by Abraham Howard. When Abraham's brother Jesse took over that mill, he used so much water that John Stringer could only run his waterwheel at night. In 1800, John Stringer became bankrupt and the mill he leased was sold to Peter Marsland. Following a dispute between Jesse Howard and Peter Marsland over water use, Howard built a wall across the reservoir. As the tunnel was on Howard's side of the wall, Marsland's water supply dried up. In response, Marsland built Nab Weir farther upstream in Woodbank Park, and also a tunnel which entered his side of the reservoir. He also built a tunnel parallel to the ACMT that fed his mills in the Park. Stringer's Tunnel originally had twists, perhaps where workers had avoided black mud to make digging easier. It was straightened and lined with sprayed-concrete by the CEGB in 1957–58.

There is a large sluice gate at river level, upstream of the weir, which is housed in a brick chamber. A shaft at the back provides access to the tunnel behind it. Graffiti shows that people have entered the chamber, though it's likely few have ventured down into the smelly, muddy hole beneath it.

Having seen photos, we knew that exploring the tunnel was possible, however we were concerned about air quality, given the possibility of organic waste producing hydrogen sulphide. Finding out there was airflow between an access shaft and the entrance would be the reassurance we needed to plan a trip. A few weeks earlier, Lee and I had gone to check it out. By the side of New Zealand Road is a large, metal-

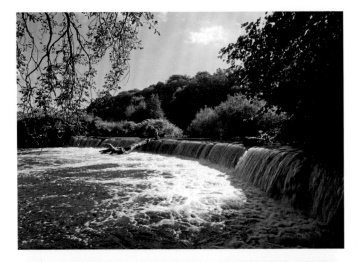

Stringer's Weir.

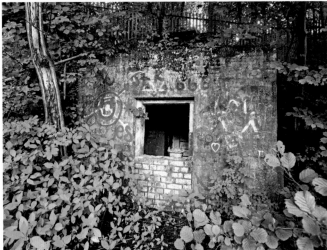

Stringer's Weir sluice
chamber.

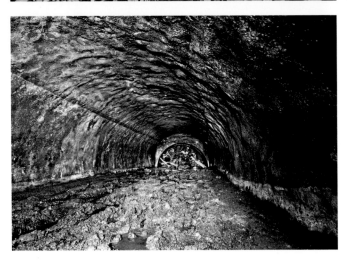

Stringer's Tunnel
entrance.

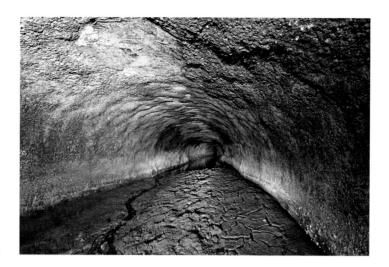

Heading into
Stringer's Tunnel.

lidded, concrete-lined shaft descending into the tunnel. The shaft was sunk in 1957, over seven days in twelve-hour shifts. It is securely sealed but a tiny hole in the bricks enabled us to drop a plumb line down. We unravelled the weighted string until the line went loose, then tied a knot in it. Peering into the hole, I felt a strong, warm breeze on my eye, rising out of the tunnel. We pulled the string up and laid it out on the pavement to measure and visualise it: this shaft was 20 metres deep.

Dan, Lee, Matt and I prepared for a trip. We expected to get very wet and very dirty. We wanted to travel as far as possible, and of course take photographs, so the right kit was essential. The first section, heading west under Vernon Park, is filled with deep, sticky mud. The tunnel is almost fully submerged farther on. Having found waders heavy and inflexible, and downright dangerous if water gets inside them, I went for just a wetsuit and wetsocks, for ease of movement. We packed cameras, spare torches, gloves, walking sticks, lilos, and dry-bags – which make a good buoyancy aid when sealed with air inside. We descended the ladder in the sluice chamber, crawled over filthy debris, and stood for the first time in The Beast. It was impressively huge – at least 2 metres high and over 2 metres wide.

The Beast really was as challenging as we expected. Every step was a fight to release our feet from its grasp while struggling to remain upright. Along the sprayed-concrete walls are regular holes which drain ground water into the tunnel. There were two tidemarks: one around our knees, which was made by the current flow of water (mostly from the drainage holes, rather than the river), and one closer to the ceiling which shows the height of water when the tunnel was opened to the river. Underneath the west side of Vernon Park is an old access shaft into Stringer's Tunnel, capped with a rusty plate. This shaft was sunk in 1878 to facilitate repairs to a collapsed roof section. We then came to the enormous New Zealand Road shaft. Standing underneath, we heard voices and the sounds of gardening as clearly as if we were right next to the people working far above us.

The next stretch is wider and drier. Trickling water has carved a narrow channel between dry, sandy banks. This is where we took measurements of water flow with a litre jug and a stopwatch. On two occasions, it measured 12 litres per minute, and once, after a few days of dry weather, just 3 litres per minute. I will come back to the reason for taking measurements later.

We reached the point where the first part of Stringer's Tunnel used to end – at Howard's Reservoir. In 1957 the reservoir was filled in and the water culverted in concrete pipes to

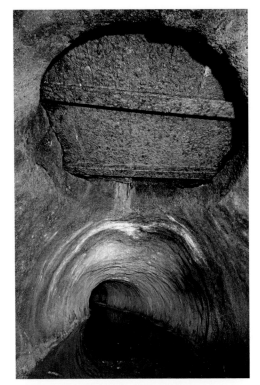

Vernon Park shaft.

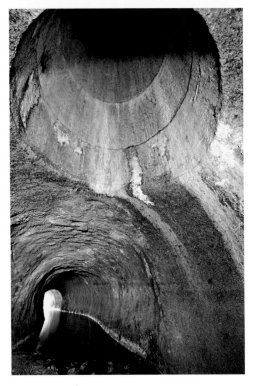

New Zealand Road shaft.

supply Millgate Power Station. The reinforced concrete pipe (RCP) is considerably smaller than the original tunnel. Old photographs show an access shaft from outside, encased in a concrete box. The surface is now industrial land divided between Wheatley Plastics and Manufax. Stringer's Tunnel, both the sprayed-concrete sandstone and RCP sections, lies just 4 metres below the surface. The new shaft can't be accessed from above since it lies in the old mill, which is now a working factory.

There are several larger reservoir outflows, all blocked at source or on the riverbank, which can be seen from St Mary's Way Bridge. Not all of the arches are tunnel exits; some are just supporting the wall. One of the exits is named Dirty Duck. This large tunnel discharged water from Howard's reservoir into the Goyt. A few years ago, its backfill was excavated by some determined explorers. Working in cramped conditions, it took them many months to clear a low passage just 15 metres long. They eventually found it was blocked by concrete and no longer led to the tunnel system.

Beyond the reservoir (underneath Newbridge Lane) the tunnel joins one branch of the ACMT. It is also over 2 metres high and 2 metres wide. As it heads deeper underground the water level rises. We floated in pairs on lilos, punting slowly forward by pushing against the walls. No outside noises made their way down here, the only sounds were the rough scraping of gloves on stone, rhythmic sloshing of water around us, and deep, heavy breathing as we surveyed this unexplored territory. The cold water, undisturbed for decades, was crystal clear. My legs dangled over the lilo but were in no danger of touching the ground. I looked down. The water looked almost blue. Silt and sand had long since settled in a thin layer on the bottom. I lowered my oar and didn't even come close to touching the bottom. A rusty pipe hung from the roof and under it delicate flakes of rust dropped, then paused, before slipping beneath the surface. We pushed on until the air became still and steamy, and our heads bumped on the roof. When there was no

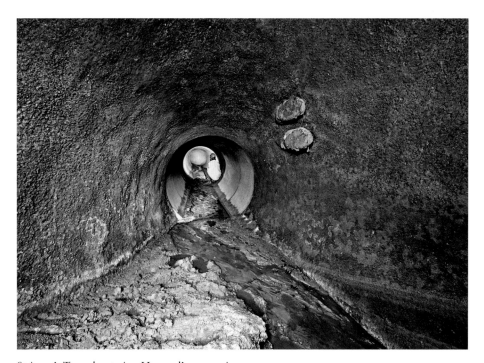

Stringer's Tunnel entering Howard's reservoir.

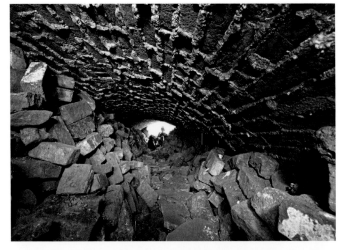

Dirty Duck.

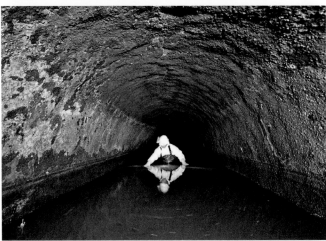

Under Newbridge Lane.

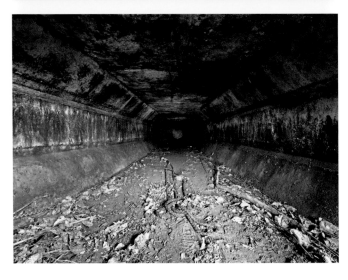

Power station surge pipe.

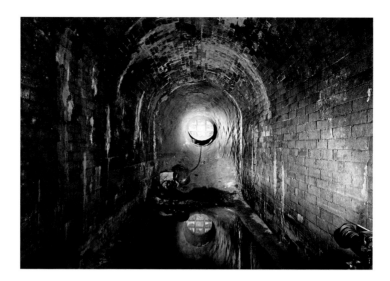

Power station
valve door.

longer enough space to sail any further, we turned around and began the long journey back out.

The Newbridge Cut

In the woods by the River Goyt are two sealed access shafts similar to, but smaller than, the shaft at New Zealand Road. They indicate the start of the Newbridge Cut – a narrow reservoir, now filled in. We guessed that one of them led to the ACMT from Howard's reservoir, the other to the parallel, disused second ACMT but didn't yet know which was which. We had first talked about draining Stringer's Tunnel a few years ago. Back then we didn't know how much water was in there, just that somewhere between Howard's reservoir and Stockport it was completely filled, for an unknown distance.

Between the narrow crack in the covers of Newbridge Cut Chamber One we could see water and assumed this was our flooded tunnel. We ran a hosepipe into the river and siphoned out several tons of water until the levels equalled and just under 1 metre remained in the 3-metre shaft. This revealed a ladder and two valve wheels, but no tunnel.

On the brick wall by the riverbank was a pipe at ground level, and a lidded exit a few feet above it. Both were half filled with mud and most likely came from Chamber One. Opening the valves might drain the whole tunnel easily, but could also let the river in to fill it up again. We decided to only try it as a last resort. Chamber Two was a dry shaft with a metal lid around 2 metres below ground level. This could also be our tunnel. Unfortunately, it was half covered by a large fallen tree, limiting our view and making it impossible to prod the lid. Meanwhile, Lee and Matt had discovered an entrance which could prove to be the answer to the problem.

Millgate Power Station opened in 1898 and was situated by the Goyt on the present Millgate car park. It was a coal-fired station until 1963, when it converted to oil. By 1958, Stringer's Tunnel had been restored to provide water for the power station. Intake to it was controlled by a large metal door which could be lowered to close off flow from the tunnel. To relieve pressure when the door was closed, a surge pipe was constructed that allowed water to spill out into the river. We crawled into the surge pipe entrance – a 1-metre-high rectangular concrete tunnel. It was filthy: lined with fine soot which settled in our pores, fingernails, and clothes so we looked like coal miners after every visit. Around 10 metres in, it becomes 1 metre RCP and inclines steeply downwards. I was scared upon first contemplating this drop, imagining slipping uncontrollably down and being unable to climb back out again. I couldn't see whether the bottom was wet or dry. We tied a rope to three rusty bars at the entrance, hoped they would hold, and slid into the abyss. I fell out of the pipe onto a pile of wet, dirty gravel, relieved to be on solid ground rather than in several feet of water.

A small stream of water flowed from the left (Newbridge Cut) to the right (power station). This gave us a possible end point for the flooded section of the tunnel beyond the reservoir. Stooping uncomfortably, we walked along the 5-foot RCP to the left and covered some sixty sections (around 2.5 metres each in length) before the water was in danger of breaching our waders. A fine crust of mineral deposits coated the undisturbed surface, cracking into fragile flakes as we moved through it. Pushing a wave of water produced an echoing bang, presumably from the water slapping the roof of the pipe, or a wall at the end. Shouts bounced back as high-pitched whistles. We had two possibilities: was this the sump of an open tunnel from the reservoir, or was it sealed at the Newbridge Cut?

To the right of the surge pipe was a small gap under a thick, circular, metal door. It was rusted in place (we hoped) and had a metal bar propping it open. We lay on our backs and shimmied under it as quickly as possible. I must have done it at least twenty times since that first visit, but each one felt like it could be my last. I made it through, still alive, and scrambled to my feet on the other side. For the past few years I had stooped and crawled through tiny, filthy tunnels and become used to the idea that this small town only had small tunnels. I was so wrong, and now, so happy. We were in a beautiful arched tunnel, measuring 2 by 3 metres. The walls were blackened brick that had skinny white calcite straws hanging from the ceiling and clear, shallow water covered the brick floor. The tunnel curved away into the darkness.

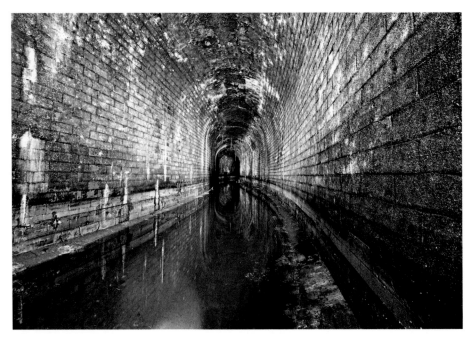

Power station tunnel.

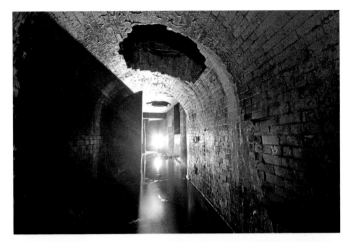

Hole in the roof of
power station tunnel.

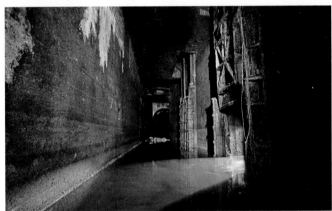

Power station suction
chamber doors.

Water trickled through the door yet the level was low, so this tunnel must still drain into
the river. We waded in, disturbing dark clouds of ancient silt. Sounds of water dripping and
pouring into the tunnel, from between cracks in the bricks, echoed off the walls. Our voices
boomed back at us. We sloshed along towards the power station basement. We passed
under some large holes in the roof which had been filled in from above. The rubble in
them looked precarious so I didn't stand underneath them for long. One had a pile of glass
and glazed bricks underneath it – remnants of the power station building. Another had a
circular wooden lid valiantly holding up piles of stones. It corresponds to a sinkhole in the
pavement above, in Millgate car park, which was recently filled in with tarmac.

Then we saw the sluice doors: 3-metre-high, thick metal doors, now rusted and
flaking, and stuck forever in the last positions they had held. It felt like discovering
evidence of an ancient civilisation. There were five, on two sides of a rectangular
concrete structure – the suction intake. Behind each door was a small chamber with a
hole on the back wall (measuring 1 metre in diameter) covered by a metal plate, which
looked like a giant sieve. We presumed them to be for filtering dirty water that had
come from the river. A final huge door, fortunately for us stuck open with a small gap
at the bottom, would have sealed the entire tunnel. This door would be closed to raise
the water level for intake into the chambers. The circular tunnel to the side has been
backfilled with tons of rubble. It used to lead to a short section of tunnel which was
once part of the ACMT.

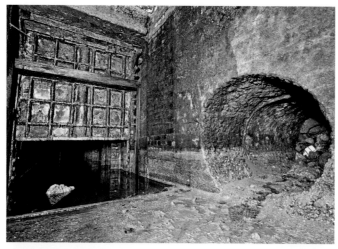

Power station door
and discharge tunnel.

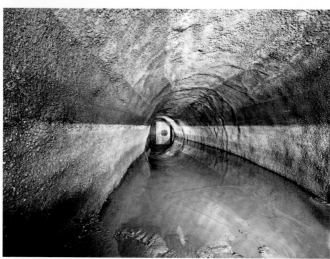

Power station tunnel
towards the Park.

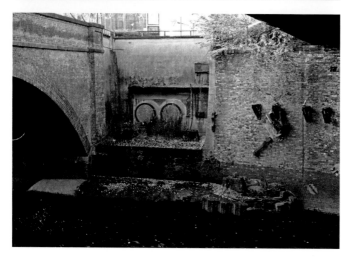

Millgate Bridge, power
station water pipes,
and tunnel exit.

Beyond it, the ACMT is spray-concreted sandstone again, and heads towards the Park. At the end of the power station it continues ahead, but is sealed by a securely bolted metal plate. There are stone steps leading out of the water on the left. Water flows out to the river through a low tunnel on the right. Changing water levels can be seen in the tidemarks on the walls. We waded in and the ground sloped away sharply. By the time we got to the end it was chest deep and bracingly cold. We stumbled up the steps into a narrow and stoopy dry-sandstone tunnel. It headed back in the direction we had just travelled. After a short distance a brick wall halted our progress. I later found out that it ends just beyond the wall, and was a 'discharge chamber'.

We went to investigate the exit tunnel. I took a deep breath and swam over, sinking up to my nose in the chilly water to peer in. There was just a few inches of airspace so I couldn't enter. It was a short sandstone tunnel; no daylight shone through from the end. We later saw from outside that it is bricked up. There must be a gap in the bricks to let the water out. It enters the Goyt just below Millgate weir. There's a protective outer wall but, when the river is high, water can't leave the tunnel, and may even wash back in. The pipes, which can be seen on either side of Millgate Bridge, took water to and from the cooling towers on the opposite bank. The first two cooling towers were wooden. Harry told me the construction workers were Danish. I asked him why they built cooling towers from wood, he supposed it was to get them up quickly. A concrete tower followed in 1943 and dominated the skyline until its demolition in 1981.

Jim Clare told me that when he was a boy he went on a school trip to the power station. His group were taken down a spiral staircase into the basement, and along a large tunnel which was dry, lit and had cables running along it. They walked for some way and were then told they were standing underneath Vernon Park. At that time there was no completely intact water tunnel to Vernon Park. I don't doubt his account, but we looked and couldn't find it on any map. I am still looking for it.

We had gone as far as we could from both ends of the tunnel, but couldn't leave it at that. The possibility of being the first (in fifty years) to do a through trip was enticing. We started to seriously consider emptying the tunnel. It wouldn't do any harm – we would only be returning water to the river it had come from. In fact, it was already flowing there by itself; we just needed to make it flow out a bit faster than it flowed in.

At first we only had one garden hose, around 20 metres long. We secured it under the water in the RCP with a brick and took the other end through the circular door into the

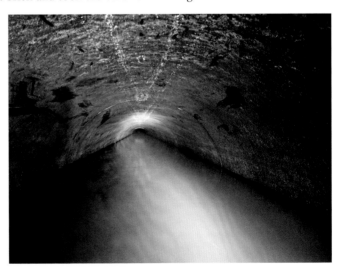

Newbridge Cut Tunnel
before draining.

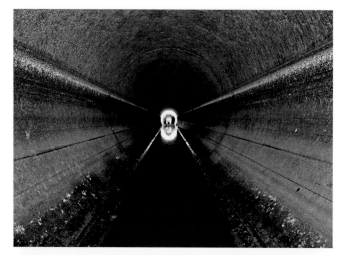

Newbridge Cut Tunnel
after draining.

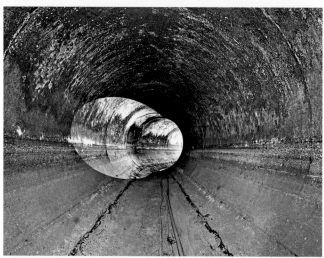

Dry Newbridge Cut
Tunnel.

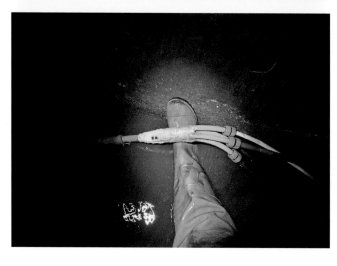

Dan's Manifold.

brick tunnel. After a minute or two of hand pumping, sandy water started running out of the hose. It flowed at 10 litres a minute, hopefully more than what was flowing in upstream. We left it for four days and went back in to check on progress. It had worked. The water's edge had retreated down the pipe. Unfortunately, this had exposed the end of the hose and drainage had stopped.

We did some maths and estimated that the tunnel contained around 3,600 tons (360,000 litres) of water. Although we were siphoning out 10 litres per minute, we didn't know how fast water was coming in. We had an average figure (from measuring in Stringer's Tunnel) of 9 litres per minute coming in, therefore only 1 litre a minute going out. At that rate it would take eight months of constant siphoning to empty completely. We only needed to remove enough to get past the sump, but we didn't know how deep that was. At this point we didn't even know if the tunnel was blocked, or open all the way to Vernon Park.

Over the next few months we bought and borrowed four more garden hoses and a fire hose, joining them up as the water lowered and moved farther away. The siphon stopped regularly. Heavy rain filled the tunnel back up over and over. It seemed an impossible task.

In desperation, we decided to try to open the Newbridge Cut valve. It was like a kind of keyhole surgery, working 2 metres down, through a 2-centimetre gap in the metal covers. Dan attached a skyhook to a cord and lowered it in. I pushed against the cord with a tent pole to place the skyhook over the valve wheel. It clanked against the wheel, but failed to catch. Several tries later we managed to hook the wheel and pulled. It moved! We carefully repeated the manoeuvre. Dan managed to hook and pull the wheel a few times but it moved less than one full turn before sticking. We waited, but nothing happened. Back to the drawing board.

The obvious answer was to use a big pump. Lee had one which would pump several tons a minute. The problem was, it needed power and we couldn't run a generator underground because of the fumes. We couldn't run it overground either: even if we had the 100 metres of cable it would require, the noise would draw too much attention. Lee and Matt came up with another idea: a small but powerful battery-powered pump. They hauled two car batteries and the pump components into the tunnel, building the pump in situ. The battery sat on a couple of car tyres just above the water. The pump would run for eight hours, draining 30 litres a minute. Once the battery ran out, the siphon should carry on working.

We went back a couple of days later to change the battery. We walked past the first hose, now unused, lying in mud. Past the next one, also out of the water. This was the lowest level yet. We attached the second battery and restarted the pump. A day later and the water had lowered even more. For the first time the sand at the beginning of the RCP was dry. Dan pushed a wave along the water, but a moment later we heard the familiar slap and a bang: it was still hitting something. Maybe the tunnel really was bricked up at the Newbridge Cut.

A few days later Lee brought a recharged battery and we started the pump for the third time. It was about a week before we could go back and check up on it, and during that time it had been raining so we weren't hopeful. Our waves slap-banged the end again. We decided to wade as far as possible and see if we could see anything new. Dan had been marking numbers on the pipe walls. We had reached Section 75 previously, this time we reached 90 before we were chest deep. Floating among the white flakes on the surface was something new: rusty debris we hadn't seen before. Where had it come from? It could only be from the other side of the sump. We must have briefly dropped the level just enough to allow these bits to float through, then the water had risen back up.

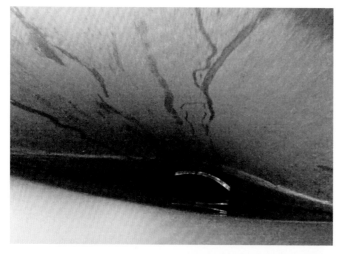

Approaching Newbridge Cut valve chamber.

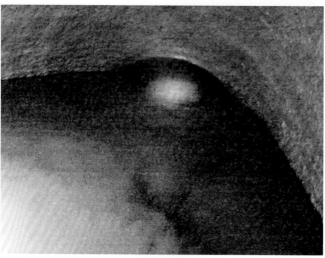

Stringer's Tunnel meeting Newbridge Cut Tunnel.

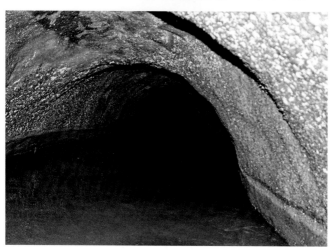

Stringer's Tunnel before draining.

It was an encouraging sign. However, by now we had reached the end of our hoses, and it seemed we would never move the water faster than it filled up. Fortunately, Dan was determined to continue. He extended the siphon length by making a manifold to feed the smaller hoses into the bigger one. He monitored water levels and restarted the siphon up to twice a week for several months. One evening we went for a quick check on the siphon, aiming to be in and out between the hourly chimes of St Mary's bells. We shuffled into the pipe and squatted at the bottom, unpacking our bags. Suddenly, we stopped and looked at each other, 'Do you feel that?' 'Yes!', it was a faint, but constant, cool breeze blowing from the left. We had made a breakthrough.

Dan and I came back ready to get wet. It was now or never. There wasn't the half a metre, comfortable clearance I would have liked but, after so much work, we had to seize this chance. I wouldn't be able to use a camera on a tripod so Dan strapped a head-cam to his helmet. We bent over and trotted down the RCP to the now distant water's edge, where I left my coat and wellies and stepped in. We walked past Sections 60 ... 75 ... 90, sinking lower into the cold water. Dan leaned on his inflated dry-bag, I gripped a pool noodle in each hand. We half waded, half swam. The pipe inclined at a steeper angle, but with no external references it was difficult to see that – instead it felt like we were in a horizontal pipe that was slowly filling with water. As the level rose, or rather, we descended deeper into the sump, my helmet scraped the roof and water lapped against my chin. Only our heads and hands remained above water. I was hoping this would be as deep as it got but no, the pipe kept going down. I tilted my head to the side, right ear submerged, nose and mouth just above the water. Concentrating on breathing slowly and deeply, I cautiously pushed on. Ahead, Dan had stopped and stood up – he had reached the Newbridge Cut. I squeezed in next to him and rose out of the water with relief.

We were in a 2-metre shaft that was barely wide enough for two people, and guessed we were at the bottom of Chamber Two. Immediately above our heads was a bolted metal lid. Dan said he thought we were nearly through. He ducked into the pipe again and kept going. I leaned on my noodles and watched him float for approximately 10 metres when he then shouted back, 'I'm in a huge tunnel!'. He said he was looking at an enormous sandbank in a 4 by 3-metre tunnel, and that it could be damming water upstream. We decided not to wade in and disturb it in case we released a deluge which would submerge our exit. It didn't matter about turning back now, we had made it. The photograph shows the pipe emerging into the cavernous Stringer's Tunnel.

The final part of this mission had to be a return visit to the other end of the tunnel, to see how far we could get now that the water was lower. We waited for a nice sunny day, so that when we emerged, wet and muddy, we could dry off on the way back to the car. This time we travelled light, bringing just a lilo and a headcam. I took off my boots and left them on the surface; climbing down the ladder in my wetsocks was uncomfortable. I remembered that the last two rungs were rusted and broken, so I hung and lowered myself off the fourth rung until my toes felt the spongy ground. I stepped cautiously into the dirty, silky mud. At first it seemed nothing had changed – the sludge was just as sludgy, water still trickled through the walls, and landmarks like sandbanks looked exactly the same as last time. Then we passed through Howard's reservoir. We left the RCP and entered the lowest section of the old tunnel, crawling until it opened up. Perhaps the water had receded a little. It was shallow enough to wade a little farther than before. When we reached the final sandbank before deep water, we stopped to inflate the lilo, pressing the foot pump against the wall.

We held an oar each and wordlessly coordinated our paddling to keep the lilo on an even course. The tidemark might have been a little higher, I couldn't remember. Dan was filming, so I barely spoke to allow him to capture the eerie sounds: the plunge, drag, splash, and drip of every oar-stroke; the occasional jarring scrape of plastic on sprayed concrete; and faint echoes of shallow breathing.

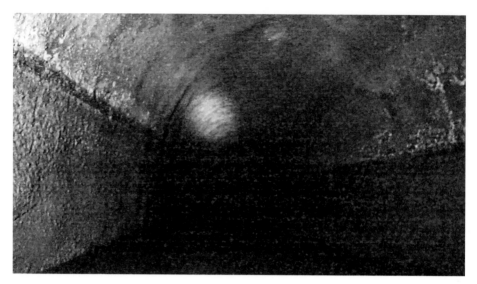

Stringer's Tunnel after draining.

The roof got lower but we paddled on, leaning forward until Dan was horizontal and I was pressing my face into his back. My legs trailed loosely in the deep water. Suddenly, the roof rose and the walls widened. We sat up slowly and found ourselves in a 4-metre-wide chamber. It was smooth, round and sandy coloured, with a rusty tidemark above the water line. This was it – the end of Deep Silt and the beginning of the Newbridge Cut. The water level had dropped, but risen again as soon as we stopped siphoning. The pipe Dan had walked out of was so deep below us we couldn't even see it. The images show the difference in water level – nearly 2 metres.

Marsland's Tunnels

In 1811 Peter Marsland built a tunnel from Nab Pool, part of the River Goyt on his estate, to Woodbank Reservoir, later known as Swan Pool, and the Nine Foot Tunnel from there to his mill on Newbridge Lane. By 1819 he had built a low weir which extended just halfway across the river below the tunnel. He completed a second, larger weir across the whole river in 1833. The original weir is still there, just under the water, above the current Nab Weir. From the weir to Howard's reservoir, the tunnel (broken by Swan Pool) measures just over 1,100 metres.

Nab Tunnel's entrance is buried underground. All that can be seen on the surface is the top of a brick archway which would be for the sluice control. The tunnel faces upstream and heads straight across the first loop in the river. There are three outlets in Woodbank Park: Ice House Sluice, a waste weir, and Swan Pool overflow.

The first outlet to Nab Tunnel, the Ice House Sluice, is in a small crevasse under the riverside path. A map from 1910 shows a capstan (winding mechanism) above it for lifting the gate. The only remaining capstan I have seen is the one on Newbridge Lane.

In 2009, Horus and I explored part of the tunnel. Between the Ice House Sluice and Swan Pool is a waste weir which would have let water out to the river when the gate to Swan Pool was closed. Under the 2-metre-wide brick archway is a narrow gap filled with leaves and cobwebs. Not knowing much about it, other than it was flooded, we just dived in, dragging our camera bags, and *Debbie*, behind us. We slid down the mudbank

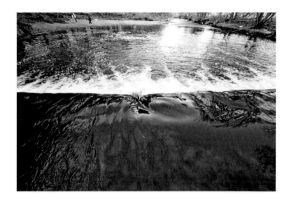

Nab Weir.

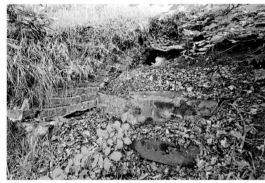

Nab Tunnel entrance.

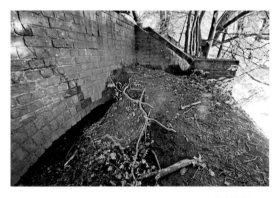

Marsland's waste weir.

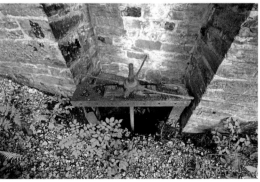

Capstan near Howard's Mill on
Newbridge Lane.

into a wide sandstone chamber. To the right (west) were slots for an almost 2-metre-wide sluice gate, then a muddy, cut-and-cover, brick tunnel; to the left (east), a smooth sandstone tunnel half-filled with water.

We went right first because it looked like there was solid ground to crawl on. After a few metres we realised it wasn't solid at all. The mud was so saturated we started to sink if we paused for even a moment. Lying down, we managed to spread our weight and stay afloat long enough to take a couple of photographs. Moving on, the mud rose until there wasn't even space to carry bags. I offered to go on to find the end and Horus waited. I lay flat and squirmed along the slippery surface. Feathery roots adorned with water droplets hung between every brick, twinkling prettily in our torchlight. Eventually, I could go no further – the mud was too high. I turned and slid back to Horus. We later realised it ended where Swan Pool was filled in.

We inflated *Debbie* and set sail in the other direction. We paddled slowly, inspecting every pebble and scratch on the walls. We could see what looked like the end – it must be the Ice House Sluice intersection. As we approached, *Debbie* ran aground. What had looked like water was actually very wet silt – impossible to wade through, or sail on. We pushed against the walls, shifting and rocking to move the boat forward. Rather like doing a sack race, on your knees, with two people in the sack. We were within metres of the intersection when we noticed a smell in the air – eggs, meaning hydrogen sulphide. This poisonous gas has the effect of numbing your ability to smell it. We knew that even if we stopped smelling it, it could still be there in greater concentration. The Nab Weir end of the tunnel was a dead end – unventilated. It could be filled with hydrogen sulphide. There was no hesitation; we immediately turned around and hurried back to the entrance.

The Ice House Sluice outlet is bricked up, with two 15-centimetre pipes through the bricks which drain when the water level rises, keeping the depth inside at around 1 metre. There is usually a constant flow, so water is still getting in somewhere. A few years later, Dan and I could still smell hydrogen sulphide when we looked into these pipes. We pondered how to ventilate the tunnel. Making a little hole at Nab Weir might do it, but the tunnel entrance is deep underground and we couldn't really start digging in the park. The

Marsland's tunnel looking west.

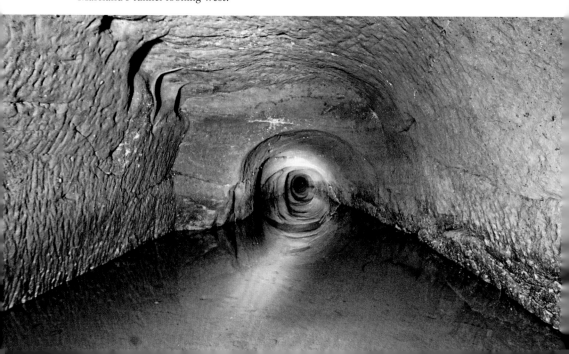

next idea seemed better: block the Ice House Sluice until Nab tunnel filled with water all the way to the waste weir, then release it. As the water rushed out, it would draw fresh air back into the tunnel. We called it Operation Gas Blast.

Dan made two cylindrical plugs from expanding foam. We squeezed them into the pipes, covered them with mud, and left them for a week. Dan was concerned that the plugs wouldn't withstand the pressure of so much water behind them. Hopefully no one would take a look at the pipes in the meantime. The plugs could be ejected with a great deal of force at any point; it was a dripping time bomb.

When we returned we checked the level at the waste weir. It might have gone up a little, but we hadn't taken photos before we started so it was hard to tell for sure. It could take weeks, or even months to see a result – would the plugs hold for that long? We were relieved to find them intact and just a tiny stream of water leaking out. I thought they had moved a little, so pushed one back in. I pushed too hard and it went right through, bobbing up to the surface inside. Tons of water gushed out onto me. We watched dejectedly for a few minutes. It was still gushing when we left.

On reflection, we decided that hydrogen sulphide would also be in the silt (which we couldn't remove), having been dissolved in the water. It would be released by disturbing the silt, so we abandoned the operation.

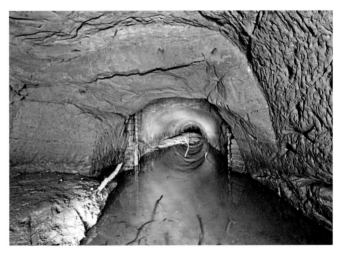

Marsland's tunnel looking east.

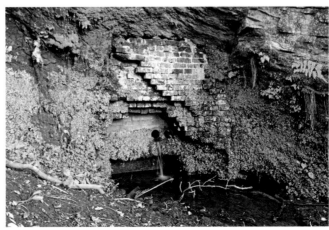

Ice House Sluice.

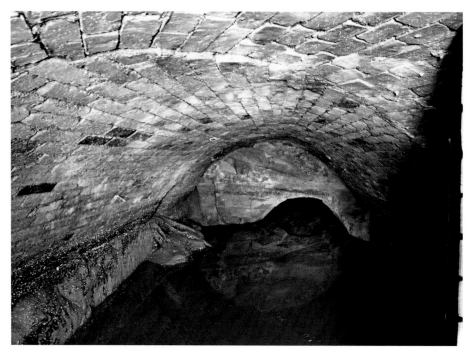

Feeder for the Nine Foot Tunnel.

Tithe maps from around 1850, during Henry Marsland's ownership, call Swan Pool Reservoir 'Shootley's Pool', and the large pond up in Woodbank Park 'Swan Pool', but the name Swan Pool seems to have stuck with the lower reservoir. The Marsland family had a boathouse in this area. Swan Pool had an overflow channel, the concrete remains of which can be seen by the riverbank. The reservoir was filled in after a tragic event in the 1940s: Jim Clare and his siblings were playing here when his sister fell in and drowned.

The Nine Foot Tunnel, which took water from Swan Pool to the Newbridge Lane mills, was completed in 1826. The CEGB mapped its approximate line but didn't explore it, due to it being silted up. The entrance is deep under Woodbank Park. It was buried when Swan Pool was filled in. An old ventilator pipe marks the junction between the Nine Foot Tunnel and a 6-foot side loop. It is still visible on the hillside near Stringer's Weir.

The tunnel ends at a gauge basin, once connected to Howard's reservoir. When the current Manufax engineering workshop was built a few years ago they found what were described as culverts under the property. These were the end of Nab Tunnel and feeder tunnels. I asked an employee and he confirmed an old tunnel was found, which is now underneath their car park. This is the closest we got to the Nine Foot Tunnel, the connecting tunnel from the gauge basin. The rest of them are inaccessible, if not completely filled in. The cavern roof is 3 metres underground. I was wearing waders so lowered myself slowly into the water, not knowing how deep it was. Hanging off the brick ledge I wiggled my feet around but couldn't feel the bottom – this meant the cavern was at least 3 metres high. From this position I couldn't see far into the tunnel but was pretty sure it was a dead end at the now-filled gauge basin.

In 1808, Peter Marsland bought land in Portwood for a large reservoir. The reservoir was filled by two 2-metre-diameter tunnels which ran underneath the Goyt, from the ACMT, using waste water from the Newbridge Lane mills. Another tunnel under the river at Park Bridge took the water from Portwood reservoir to King Street Mill in the Park. It is claimed that in 1825 Isambard Kingdom Brunel built the first tunnel in the world under a navigable river (the Thames), but it could be argued that Peter Marsland beat him to it. The reservoir later became a boating lake and advertised 'Five Splendid Boats ... an elegant Cutter, a ship's life boat, a swift Racing Craft – formerly a Captain's gig, a swift cutter and *The Alma*, an elegant Yacht Punt'. In the 1870s it was filled in and became the site of a new gasworks and a cattle market. The area now includes the Peel Centre retail park, Matalan, and gas holders.

Fernley Gully and Binns' Deep

Water tunnels west of Merseyway were not surveyed, so we had to guess their origins by consulting old maps and exploring them for possibly the first time since their excavation.

There was a late-nineteenth-century weir west of Wellington Bridge (Wellington Weir); its remains are just visible at low water from the bus station and the bridge. Above the weir are two holes. When I saw them I knew they had to be water tunnels. I avoid wading if there's a better alternative, but here it would be much easier than sailing or climbing: there's nowhere to moor a boat and this part of the Mersey is full of rubble and it's shallow, therefore fast. I waited until it had been dry and sunny for several days and waded across the remains of the weir. As I crossed, even at this midsummer low level, the river got deeper until it reached my thighs and pushed persistently against my waders. I planted my feet firmly until I reached the safety of the south bank. Here I saw, to my left, Fernley Gully – a low brick archway, filled almost to the top with silt and crowned with a heavy fringe of ferns. Clear water flowed out; I guessed it once discharged waste water, possibly from Wellington Mill, and now drains rainwater or

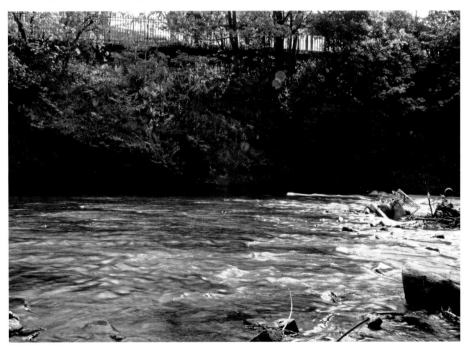

Entrances to Fernley Gully and Binns' Deep.

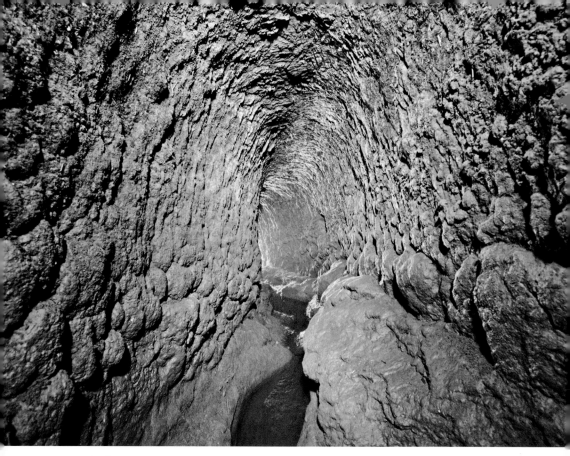

Inside Binns' Deep.

sewer overflow. To my right was Binns' Deep – a dirty sandstone tunnel. I cautiously stepped inside. The air was fresh and cool. The ground was too soft to walk on so I knelt on muddy ledges and crawled as fast as I could, curving roughly parallel to the river. I thought I might be heading for Wear Mill. Then the large tunnel seemed to end but, to my right, was a small hole. I crept in, onto a sandstone shelf in a small chamber. The tunnel did carry on, but was bricked up. I would guess it was dug from both ends, and didn't quite meet in the middle, hence the offset chamber. One small and two large drainpipes protruded through the brick wall. I could hear traffic, which I think was buses in the station above. Looking at aerial maps, the tunnel doesn't go as far as Wear Mill, so I named it after Binns' Mill which stood opposite the bus station (at the time I thought it was on the same side of the river).

Wear (Weir) Mill

In 1790, John Collier, a calico and cotton manufacturer, built a weir across the River Mersey, and to mills with wheelhouses on either side. He died in 1817 and Thomas Fernley bought the mill around 1821. After Fernley's death in 1843, the mill was worked by his son, Thomas Fernley Jr, who also had mills on Newbridge Lane. In 1846, fire destroyed the larger building (under the viaduct) and it was rebuilt with brick and iron. The smaller building was rebuilt in 1884. Apart from the half-buried base of the north bank wheelhouse, the only surviving part of Collier's mills is the south bank wheelhouse. It is Stockport's oldest industrial structure.

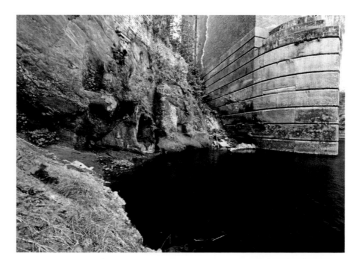

Wear Mill head race with remains of sluice gate.

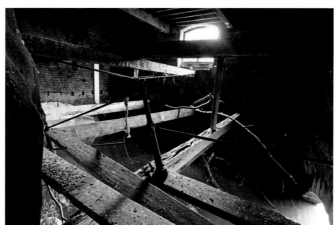

Wear Mill south bank wheelhouse.

Sandstorm

The south abutment of King Street West Bridge sits astride a 2-metre-high sandstone outcrop. Standing on the opposite bank, you can see a dark crevice in the middle, and in the shadows, a round hole. It was a hot, dry July in 2010 when I first saw it and, after some deliberation, decided to go in. I climbed down an old mill wall to the riverbank. The water was low and I was able to hop over muddy rubble to reach the bridge. The outcrop was dry, sandy on top, and smelled of foxes. I peered nervously into the hole – a circular brick tunnel around a metre in diameter. A thin trickle of water dripped from its edge and a cool breeze blew out. I crawled in, breathing hard, my heart pounding. The brick soon gave way to jagged edges of roughly cut sandstone. I was heading under King Street West. Overhead, a narrow shaft led to a manhole cover – I could hear cars bumping over it. The tunnel became smoother and lower, but I crawled on. I came to a wall, behind which I could hear rushing water, perhaps Chestergate sewer. There was a narrow gap at the top which allows for overflow. I crawled backwards until I could turn around, and squatted to take a couple of photos before I left. Sandstorm could be a tailrace from Wear Mill, but I'm not certain of that as it goes beyond the current buildings.

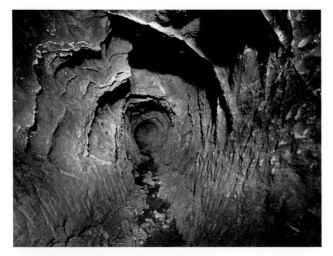

Sandstorm.

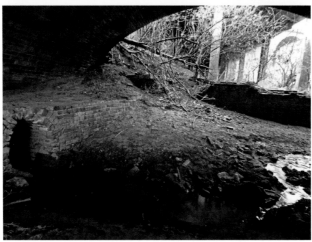

Rathole and base of
Wear Mill north bank
wheelhouse.

Rathole

Under the north abutment is a very different hole. Liam and I squatted and shuffled into this egg-shaped tunnel, presumably an old sewer. It was weathered brick all the way, ending in a tight inspection chamber somewhere under the roundabout by the Crown Inn. Drainage pipes entered from the east wall. We skidded out rapidly, our heels gliding along the slippery floor. The photograph shows the remains of a wheelhouse next to the Rathole from the mill that used to stand here, opposite Wear Mill. You can just see the top of its arch. Both Sandstorm and the Rathole can be fully submerged when the river is high.

Culverts and Sewers

If water tunnels are an adventure, sewers are an ordeal. Some people choose to explore them; the huge sewers of Manchester and London have impressive Victorian brickwork which, for more determined urban explorers than me, makes enduring the filth worth it. I had no wish to recreate *The Shawshank Redemption* but, in the pursuit of epic discoveries, often found myself ankle-deep in effluent (or 'fresh' as it is known by explorers) wondering what I was doing with my life. More than once I said, 'I am never going back in there!' only to find myself once again snapping on latex gloves and a face mask then reluctantly trudging through places that were not intended for people to trudge through. My grandma used to say, 'Why can't you take nice photos of ducks in the park?' How could I explain? The pull of the unknown was strong, and our search for new frontiers took us to some unusual places.

We didn't set out to explore sewers. They are dangerous and unpleasant. Hazards include unpredictable water levels; modern sewer systems are automatically controlled and can fill up rapidly. Even if the weather is fair locally, the system might drain storm water from another area. There are gases such as methane, which is flammable, whose presence can lower the oxygen content of the air, and pathogens such as bacteria, viruses, protozoa and worms. The preparation and cleaning up afterwards is not fun. However, as we were to discover, if you go into a culvert or old water tunnel, you're quite likely to encounter a sewer.

Before sewers and flushable toilets were invented people used outside privies, pouring soil or ash over their waste. The contents were collected and shovelled onto carts by the 'night soil' men and sent for disposal, often being used as farmland manure. The Native Guano Co. of Leamington sold dried and pressed sewage for this purpose.

Edwin Chadwick was born in Longsight in 1800 and attended school in Stockport until the age of ten. His family moved to London and he went on to become a dedicated campaigner for the reform of sanitary conditions. Chadwick was secretary to the Board of Poor Law Commissioners whose 'Sanitary Report' (1842) correlated poor living conditions with disease and death. He noted that disease was prevalent in the Heaton Norris area of Stockport. There were twenty-eight instances of public health problems from the neglect of town drainage. Stockport had outbreaks of cholera in 1832 and 1849 as a result of contaminated drinking water.

In 1840 John Roe designed the egg-shaped sewer, which was self-cleansing and efficient at maintaining flow, even at low levels. Previously, sewers were cleaned out manually, an unpleasant and unhygienic task. Roe's design was used by Joseph Bazalgette, the engineer who designed the huge London sewer network in 1865. The egg-shaped sewer design was adopted in Stockport around the same time. Chadwick worked with Bazalgette in London and they disagreed on the capacity needed, with Chadwick underestimating the size of pipes, perhaps trying to keep costs down and Bazalgette overestimating the size to allow for a growing population. Bazalgette built the system to his specifications, and he was presciently accurate. The population of London in 1850 was around 2 million; today it is over 8 million and Bazalgette's sewers are still in use. Even so, Chadwick played an important role in

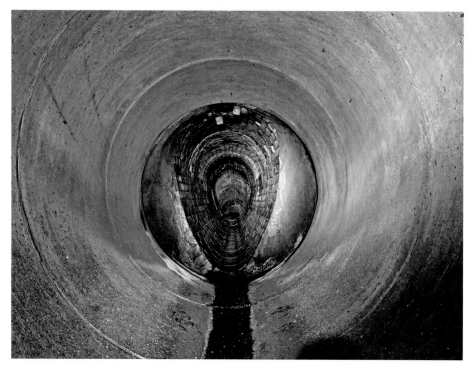

Looking into Skully.

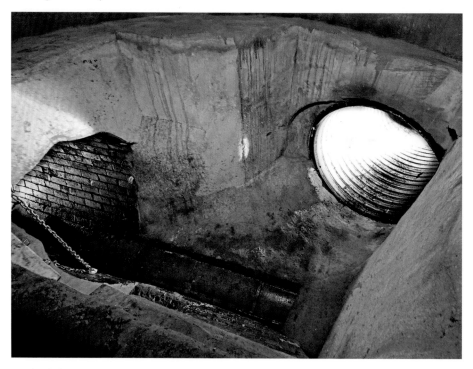

Inside Skully.

improving lives and public health and he is commemorated by a blue plaque on the house at the site of his childhood home, which can be seen on Stockport Road in Longsight.

Skully

A few years ago I climbed down to the riverbank behind Regent House to take photos under Merseyway. I rarely encounter other people when I go out, just the occasional angler or homeless person. This time, two boys climbed over the wall and watched me walking into the tunnel. They were young, maybe thirteen years old. I ignored them and carried on. They didn't speak, just started throwing stones at me. I climbed up onto the concrete abutment, thinking they wouldn't follow but they did. I squeezed behind a narrow concrete pillar as rocks hit it and landed next to me. Now I was scared they were actually going to hurt me. I was trapped. As far as I knew I was heading towards a dead end. My only advantage was having a light. I hoped I could get beyond daylight before they caught up with me. This side doesn't have a metal walkway like the south bank, and I knew the walkable part of the abutment was some distance from here. Hoping to squeeze between the walls and arches without falling into the river, I climbed over the next arch and dropped into a narrow gap between concrete walls. Stones continued to rattle on the other side. I had to go on, but fortunately it was growing darker. I scrabbled over the next arch, getting dusty and covered in pigeon droppings. Climbing up the concrete wall at the end of this section, I looked at the 3-metre drop on the other side – smooth wall, no holes; I wouldn't be able to climb back out. I had no choice but to stop here. Turning my headlight off, I sat down, silent and still, and waited. Eventually it went quiet. I waited until long after the missiles stopped landing before climbing back out to take a photo of the outlet to what would become known as Skully.

At that time I thought it was the Tin Brook outlet, but Lee and Matt later crawled in and discovered it was an egg-shaped sewer. This was quite exciting as we thought it might lead to a big, old sewer like those in Manchester. The name comes from Lee's first view from inside looking back to the slope; our lights shone up, illuminating the egg and making it look like a bright, glowing skull.

We visited a couple of times, just after a new screening chamber had been fitted. Skully is an old sewer that flows at right angles from the south and emptied directly into the Mersey until this CSO was built. It used to run over the top of Chestergate sewer, but was intercepted and now drains into the sewer rather than the river. The old sewer ascends beneath the Plaza steps to Petersgate by a series of 2-metre rises, which we didn't climb as they were slippery with effluent. As much as I liked the architecture, this was the most unpleasant place I've been in. Other sewers had smelled of shampoo, soap powder and washing-up liquid, with a just faint hint of toilets. This one was pure, undiluted human waste. I crept along cautiously, trying desperately not to slip and land face first in the stinking filth. The boys must have strong stomachs; they just laughed at me retching over the smell.

Skully didn't lead to an enormous underground complex so, interesting as it was, I was relieved that we didn't have to stay in there for much longer. As they stayed to take photos of the filter, I went back to the cleaner inspection chamber and turned off my light. I squatted and waited, listening to people outside the Plaza walking and talking above my head. I practised changing my torch batteries, blind in the dark – it's a useful skill to have. I can find my way around my house in the dark. I wouldn't like to be stuck underground with no light, but I like to think that I wouldn't be afraid.

In Stockport's early years, the local countryside was forest, marsh and farmland. Many streams trickled down to the Mersey from the high ground on both sides of the valley.

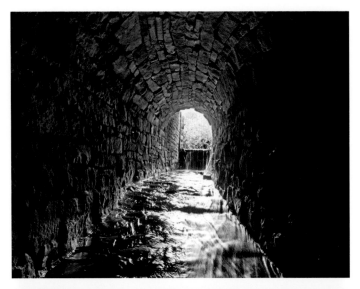

Wood Mill culvert
sluice gate.

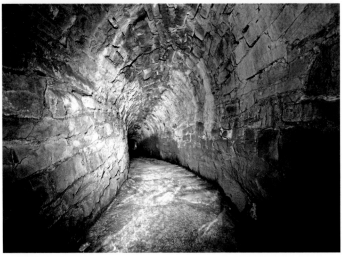

Inside Wood Mill
culvert.

Before urbanisation, rainwater had lots of open land to drain into. Once we had covered fields with houses and roads, we also had to construct a drainage system to prevent flooding. As demand for land increased, streams were culverted and built over. Stockport Council maintains sixty-two culverts. We inspected a few of them.

Wood Mill Culvert

From the early nineteenth century until it was demolished in 1964, Wood Mill in Woodley was a bone mill, woollen mill, then finally a chemical manufactory. This is the small culvert of the stream it used, which comes from Werneth Low and once filled two mill-pools before draining into the Tame. There used to be a sluice gate at the entrance to the tunnel. The brook runs under a lane to lower land on a steep incline. Not wanting to slide down into the unknown, I didn't venture far into the tunnel.

Dufresne's Ladder

Dan and Bill found this monstrosity. They enthused about it to me, saying they had found a tunnel but didn't know where it went, knowing I couldn't resist joining the investigation. As with Tunnel Two, I think I was duped. It's a hellish nightmare of endless concrete. It ruins your senses, distorting sound, light, and time. But I didn't know that at first, so agreed to go in. Dan and Bill had travelled as far as they could and stopped when they reached an obstacle. Dan and I went back to overcome it. The weather forecast looked perfect so, with an array of equipment, we waddled in. The plan was to get as far as we could, mapping along the way in order to trace the route above ground.

Through a damp, leaf-strewn woodland valley trickles a shallow brook into which crystal-clear water drains from a 5-foot RCP. It is mossy on the outside but pristine within. The front grille and, as we would later discover, one of the manhole covers and all of the access ladders had been removed, probably stolen some time ago. After 5 metres or so, we reached First Chamber. It was dimly lit from an uncovered manhole, the last glimpse of daylight we would see for the next four hours. In front of us were two pipes: a small one at ground level with water gushing out and a larger one 2 metres above it with a low wall at its exit. Climbing up, we could see that the top pipe poured water into a 'plug hole' behind the wall.

The next pipe was 1 metre high. It was worryingly clean – not a single spider or scrap of debris on the roof. That either means it never fills up, or it often does, but it was a dry day and for now the water was just inches deep. Ahead we could hear booming noises and voices ... was that a dog yelping? Maybe we were under a road. The acoustics made it impossible to tell. We crawled along rhythmically, painfully, laden with rucksacks and rope. It seemed to go on for a long time. Unable to lift my head, I had no idea how far we had travelled. Finally, we came to Second Chamber. We paused to update the map. I had no phone signal but the compass worked – we were heading south-south-east. Then it's up a level again. I took up Dan's offer of knee pads for the next stretch. My bag grew heavier and arms weaker; I felt like a pit pony, my plastic knee pads clip-clopping along the pipe.

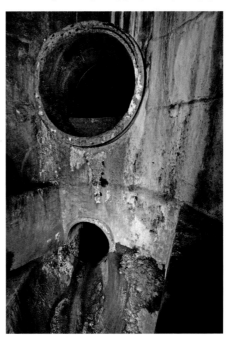

Dufresne's Ladder Chamber One.

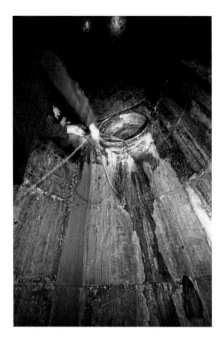

Dufresne's Ladder Chamber Four.

The clean, relentless concrete and strange sounds were starting to make me feel disoriented. We came to Third Chamber, which was another concrete box with just a rusty inlet pipe to distinguish it from the others. This time I could hear falling water and knew that the next one wasn't too far away. There was another climb up, over the wall (don't fall down the plug hole), then crawling as comfortably as possible. As I straightened up in Fourth Chamber I saw the reason for bringing all this kit. The difference between the two pipes here was considerably more than the other chambers – around 6 metres.

Dan had brought climbing gear with the intention of going up the ladder bolts, but they were far enough from the pipe for it to be a stretch for him so there was no way I'd make it. Instead, he threw the rope, weighted with carabiners, into the pipe and over the wall, bringing it rattling down the plughole. We would use single rope technique (SRT): using a hand ascender with a foot loop and a chest ascender, you slide up the rope, held by the gripping mechanism of the ascenders. We rigged and harnessed up, checking everything was clipped to where it should be. The only sounds were distant falling water and the light clicking of carabiners. It was an easy ascent, with just a little gear adjustment (adding a sling as an extra foot loop) to get over the edge. Waiting for Dan, I sat on top of the pitch and again heard strange noises which seemed to be coming from where we had just been. I realised they were our voices from moments in the past.

We threw our bags and ourselves over the plughole and crawled into the unknown. Twenty-eight sections in a south-easterly direction later, we reached Fifth Chamber. This one was very different. The walls were thickly coated in flowstone, like icing on a cake. We considered how to climb up but the fresh breeze that had followed us all the way seemed to have stopped at the entrance. The air had a faintly unpleasant smell and, with no gas tester to check it, we decided to head back. We crawled back to the pitch, made a speedy descent and packed up the now wetter, heavier gear. The return journey is a blur of pain and desperation to get out. Eventually, we tumbled into the brook, squinting at the pale sunshine and taking long, deep breaths of freedom.

We concluded this was a newish culvert, with Chambers One to Four added when a road was built over it, hence the clean, new pipes. It rises, or falls, quite steeply and, with

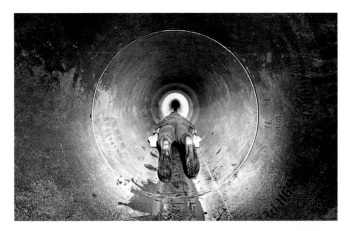

Testing the Drain Train.

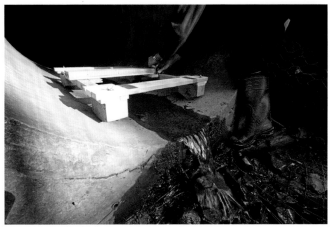

Drain Train Mark I.

its unprotected drops, is a dangerous place, which is why I have not been specific about its location. I am in no rush to revisit Dufresne's Ladder but Dan still wants to go beyond Fifth Chamber and even made a mode of transport to make the journey easier. We had a quick test run and found that friction sets fire to wooden wheels, so he took it away to make Drain Train Mark II.

Crookilley Brook

When we found a tunnel from the Goyt heading straight towards Welkin (Ark Ring) Mill, my first thought was that it must be a tail race. However, on further investigation we found that Welkin Mill, built in 1906, didn't use water in the same way as older mills. Electricity was used to drive the mill's machinery. Water for steam engines came from several boreholes under the mill, 7 inches wide and 30 to 90 feet deep. Cotton production ceased in the 1950s and it became Buckley's printers, which closed in 2008. It currently houses a paintball centre.

So, if the tunnel wasn't a tail race, what was it? I waded in to take a look from the river, but it was a bit deep and threatened to breach my waders so I couldn't get far enough to see. A boy who was watching told me that his brother had swum through the tunnel and come out on the opposite side of the river. I was dubious, but it was possible that the tunnel linked to other drainage from the motorway or old sewage works. To make room for the

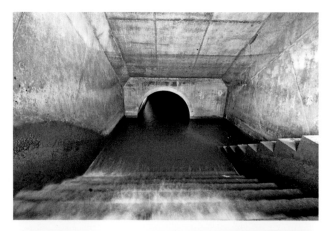

Crookilley Brook culvert
entrance.

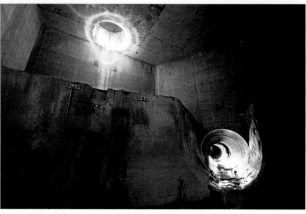

Inside Crookilley Brook
culvert.

M60, the Warth Meadow loop of the Goyt was shortened. Crookilley Brook, which had previously gone north past Welkin Mill to a sewage treatment works, was now culverted to the south in a straight line to this new exit on the Goyt.

On a bright November morning, Dan and I headed upstream, intending to follow the brook from Crookilley Wood down to the river. Its name comes from the cruck-framed house of the now demolished Crookilley Wood Farm (older spellings include Crookhilly, Cruickley, and Crookshelly). This is a medieval style of building with two pairs of curved timbers forming the roof arch. The brook rises up on the hill by Bredbury industrial estate and slowly cuts its way through soft, reddish soil. Down in the forest valley it splashes noisily into a short RCP. The brook goes underground again right next to the mill. It didn't exactly look inviting, but we had checked the weather and this was as high as it would get for now. In we go...

It was half full of silt and was therefore a stoopy struggle through boot-grabbing, sticky ground. I ventured a little way up the 1-metre side pipe before backing out, due to little fish swimming around my hands and knees. I don't like touching fish and didn't want to hurt them. Despite the Goyt being low, the exit turned out to be a lot deeper than we expected. Dan just made it to the bank on tiptoes. I slipped into the river and couldn't touch the ground. My jumper soaked up freezing water and wicked it into my waders – I later learned that's why waders should be belted. As water poured in, I frantically doggy-paddled to the edge of the outlet then grabbed the concrete wall before I was scuttled and swept downstream.

Travis Brook

A corn mill was situated by the Mersey on Travis Brook in the thirteenth century, which was at that time called Hertmillsiche – Hart Mill Brook. Hart refers to the old name for a red deer stag. Red deer were kept in parks for hunting and can still be found living wild in some parts of the country. An old road from Travis Brow to the river was called Huntsman's Brow. Roe deer, also native to Britain since Mesolithic times, still live on the outskirts of Stockport. Footage of them from cameras in woodland around Reddish Vale can be viewed in the visitor's centre.

Travis Brook Mill, designed by William Fairbairn, was built in the 1830s for Ralph Orrell's cotton spinning business. It was the largest mill in Stockport at the time. It had

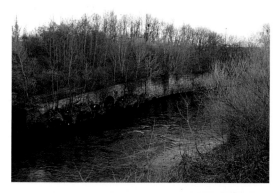

Travis Brow outlets.

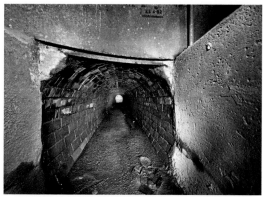

Inside Travis Brow old tunnel.

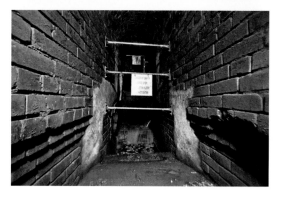

Top Rank sewer.

an octagonal chimney sited on a rocky knoll around 50 metres from the factory to keep smoke away. There was a tunnel to the chimney that is now buried beneath the motorway. There are a few holes on the north bank of the Mersey – more mill tunnels. The internal picture is of the grilled tunnel on the left. The second hole is bricked up and the third is almost fully submerged. Travis Brook is now culverted to the Mersey, passing through a CSO built in 2010 on Travis Brow. The CSO drains upstream of the third tunnel through an RCP exit.

Nearby we found a small inspection chamber which we named Top Rank. We visited on a chilly spring night and it was very old, steamy and smelly. The warmth had attracted every slug in the south Heaton Norris area and their shiny bodies lined every surface. I let Lee go in first, hoping he would 'clean' the shaft for me. It was interesting, but disgusting, inside. There was a grille in a chamber to one side with what looked like the remains of an ancient valve wheel on a penstock (to stop flow). Ahead, sewage gushed from a small inlet into a hole in the floor, solids bobbing like corks in the tumultuous waters. The sign reads, 'DANGER OF DEATH, LARGE OPEN OUTLET IN FLOOR, DO NOT ENTER.' I took two photos and scooted back up the ladder into the cold night air. I don't know for sure but guess this could be a siphon running under the river to Chestergate or Brinksway, as Cheadle sewage works are on the opposite bank of the Mersey. The only route over the river would be to follow the M60, and both this sewer and the sewage works predate that road.

Hempshaw Brook

Hempshaw Brook rises somewhere in Woodsmoor or Great Moor. The farthest I can trace it on maps is to Kennerley Road at Mile End. One day I was told there was a hole

Hempshaw Brook and Wythburn Road tributary.

in the road outside Stockport School. I went straight there on the bus and popped under a board into the hole. A small stream flowed north in an old flagstone covered culvert, possibly Hempshaw Brook itself, or a tributary. The brook flows north-west through Heaviley, Stockport Cemetery, St Thomas' recreation ground, Hope's Carr, Hillgate, and Chestergate before entering the River Mersey underneath the old clock tower in Mersey Square. It is joined, south of Hempshaw Lane, by a small tributary which rises near Wythburn Road in Heaviley and, under St Mary's Way, by Brown House Fold Brook which rises in Little Moor.

Stockport Cemetery, opened in 1838, was positioned close to Hempshaw Brook's banks and when plans to expand the cemetery towards the brook were discussed in 1856 a concerned reader wrote to the *Stockport Advertiser* stating, 'This land ... is considerably lower than the site of the Cemetery ... does it not seem probable that the drainage from the Cemetery passes through the ground, insinuating itself into the stream, which is extensively availed of for domestic consumption ... [and] infuses pernicious ingredients in that otherwise pellucid and pure stream.' By the time the cemetery expanded, the brook was enclosed in a brick tunnel beneath it. That tunnel collapsed around forty years ago. Several nineteenth-century bodies fell into the brook and had to be recovered. Under the cemetery and the old Charles Street bus depot, the pipe is now thick, bolted sections of RCP, for extra strength and to prevent leakage of pollutants into the stream.

Hempshaw Brook Brewery on Hempshaw Lane was constructed in 1835. Avery Fletcher, brewery owner and worker, dammed the brook to make a reservoir. By 1872 the brewery, then occupied by Charles Marsland, had expanded and built over the upper reservoir. The brook was encased in a pretty little brick tunnel, which gave some ingenious workers an opportunity to commit the perfect crime. With a man positioned out of sight downstream, a worker could drop bottles of beer into the brook which would float downstream to a waiting accomplice. The buildings, taken over by Robinson's in 1949 and later European

Hempshaw Brook under the old brewery.

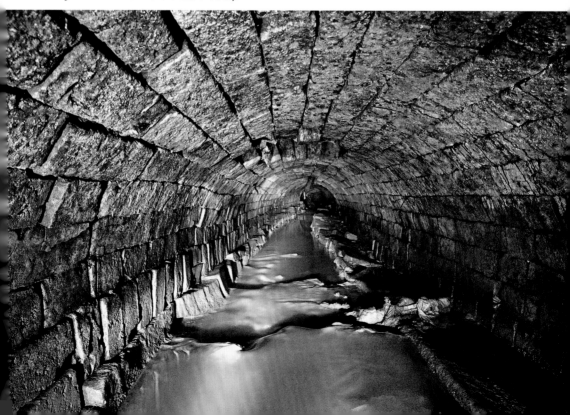

Colour Pigments, were demolished in 2012. That winter we visited the empty site late in the evening to look for access to the brook. It was snowing gently. We slipped under the fence and ran through the long shadows of construction vehicles to a dark patch in the centre of the plot – a manhole. Warmth from the culvert had melted the snow on the lid. It was a tight squeeze but somehow we managed to fit myself, Dan and Lee in there. This section was fresh and clean with lovely brickwork, softened at the edges by water and time. The brook runs clear; its colour in the photograph comes from rusty deposits stirred up by my knees. Tiny snails lined up along the water's edge. The hole in the roof could be the very one through which pilfered beer was dropped.

The brook emerges into the open by St Mary's Way. Dan and I paddled along this short section before it goes underground again by Joules Court before Waterloo Road. The water is bright orange here with iron oxide. The thick sludge we disturbed with our wellies was tar black and smelled like petrol.

Carr Brook

In the early eighteenth century the Carr was a leafy valley surrounded by farmland. Hempshaw Brook was described as a 'clear and crystal stream flowing down a pleasant valley, in which were shady walks ... [it] was crossed at Lower Hillgate by a paved way through the water for carriages and stepping stones for passengers'. The town at this time was centred around the marketplace, where you could buy and sell livestock, dairy produce and grain. Cloth was produced by local weavers in their own cottages but not yet on a large scale. Then the first silk mills were built. In 1744 an Act of Parliament was passed that allowed John Guardivaglio and George Warren to dam Hempshaw Brook and flood the upper valley. Lower Carr Mill (Stockport's second silk throwing mill after Park Mill) and the dam were built in 1759. It was still some years before the arrival of cotton. The site continued to be used in much the same way for the next two centuries.

The valley was named for Thomas Hope, who acquired Lower Carr Mill in the late 1790s and went on to create Middle and Higher Carr Mills. Hope also ordered a Boulton & Watt steam engine in 1797 for use in 'droughty weather.' In 1818, Waterloo Road was built along the southern edge of Hope's Carr, using as its foundations old gravestones removed from St Mary's churchyard when Churchgate was widened. Hempshaw Brook was taken further back and dropped down a deep brick shaft on Joules Court into a sandstone tunnel

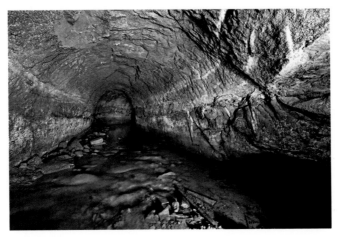

Beer Belly underneath
Waterloo Road.

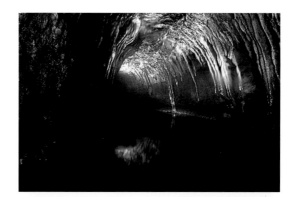

The Ribcage. (Courtsey of
D. Dawson)

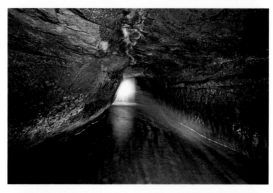

Beer Belly waterfall.

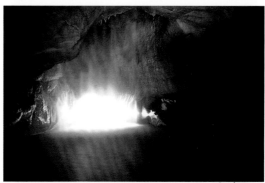

Beer Belly pool. (Courtesy of
D. Dawson)

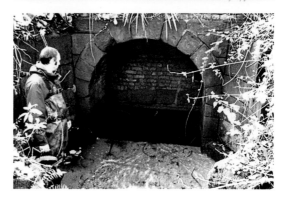

Carr Brook wheel-pit. (Courtesy of
L. Price)

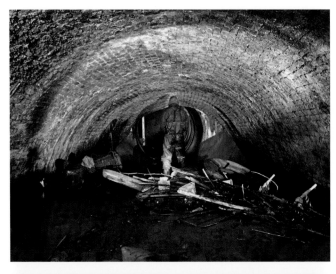

Underneath Lower
Carrs. (Courtesy of
L. Price)

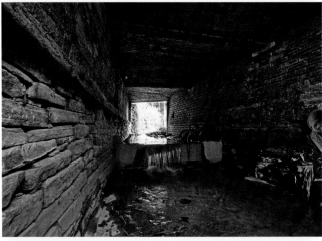

Carr Brook sluice gate.

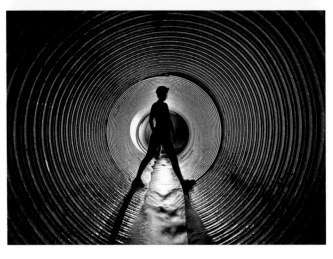

Carr Brook new pipe.

below, from where it entered the lower valley reservoir at its lowest point. In the mid-nineteenth-century the upper reservoir and surrounding fields were owned by the Rector of Stockport. An illustration shows an idyllic scene with anglers in rowing boats, the reservoir surrounded by fields and trees.

I had ventured down Tin Brook, the northern culvert from Hope's Carr, several times. It was wide open, warm and inviting. I had vague plans to look into the southern culvert but its low brick archway spewing smelly, dirty water was unappealing. However, Lee and Matt went in and discovered what is, for me, the best water tunnel in town. They didn't tell us what to expect, Lee just said, 'I think you'll like this.' Dan and I 'wadered up' and followed them in. It began with a brick tunnel. The murky water flowing out smelled faintly of petrol. As we waded upstream the water got thicker with silt and deeper. As it rose above knee level the pressure crushed my waders to my legs – a scary but comforting, grasping hug. Then we heard the unmistakable roar of falling water. It was loud and I began to feel a little nervous. The tunnel widened and a silted-up hole appeared on the right. I lifted my torch and saw curving ahead a soft, dirty, colourful tunnel around 2 metres in diameter. Looking around we noticed familiar red sandstone, green algae, high water tidemarks, sedimentary layers, shiny black spiders and sand-coloured water snails, antique debris and even older craftsmanship. I was pretty happy so far but then, rounding the next corner, we were faced with an incredible sight – jagged columns of gleaming mineral deposits. From a distance they resembled a gaping shark's mouth with layers of teeth, from within, a Geiger-esque rib cage that was simultaneously beautiful and grotesque.

At times the silt was too deep and thick to wade through so we crawled clumsily along the surface, rucksacks scraping all sorts of debris from the ceiling. The noise grew louder until we had to shout to be heard. The air was wet with spray as we reached the waterfall. It is quite spectacular – relentlessly noisy and powerful. White water thunders from a shaft, around 6 metres high, into a circular pool. I swam around behind the waterfall to light it as Dan and Lee attempted to get spray-free photographs. The pool was cold and deep; I couldn't touch the bottom. A smaller brick tunnel, filled with sand and pieces of wood,

Tin Brook under Robinson's Brewery.

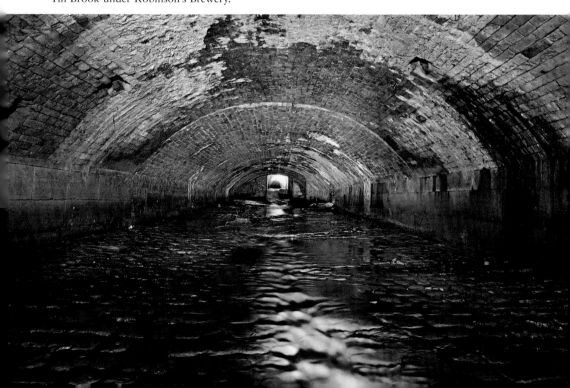

continued south, then east. A flat-out wriggle around the corner confirmed that it was blocked ahead. Its origins remain a mystery.

The lower reservoir fed Lower Carr Mill and water entered a wheel-pit through a dressed sandstone sluice. In 2013 the usual suspects, plus Simon, met up in a dimly lit car park on a cold February night. Snow started to fall. Going underground would be a welcome relief from the freezing air. We went through the familiar routine of packing dry bags, checking lights and wrapping ourselves in layers of neoprene, fleece and rubber. We slithered down the litter-strewn, ivy-coated banks of Hope's Carr and into the icy brook. The mill is now gone and just the sluice remains. Under the pretty stone archway is a shaft that drops into a downward-sloping, flagstone tunnel (the old wheel-pit). We climbed carefully down the ancient, slippery, orange walls. Once inside, we dropped to our knees as the roof descended and the water level rose. With just our head and shoulders above the dirty water, it was a wet and clumsy struggle to reach the end. We emerged from the wheel-pit into a large arched chamber (underneath the road across the valley – Lower Carrs). Until recently a small section of Carr Brook was open either side of this sluice gate behind Wellington Street. It disappeared when work began on new buildings in Hope's Carr. The sluice was removed and we found this section to be encased in 2-metre black rubber pipe which smelled pleasantly fresh, like a brand new inner tube. It felt luxurious to walk fully upright, although that wasn't to last.

Tin Brook

From here, Hempshaw Brook becomes known as Tin Brook. The name may come from the Old English *tynan*, meaning enclosed. We ducked down and entered the original culvert. Under Wellington Street it is a long, straight brick tunnel caked in mineral deposits. Beneath Robinson's Brewery is a wide, arched chamber, the end of which smells of beer. This may be the site of the ford mentioned earlier. Lots of changes in structure seem to indicate that Tin Brook was culverted in short sections at different times.

From Lower Hillgate, the culvert got smaller until we were forced to crawl, knees bruising on the cobbled surface and hands chilling in the fast-flowing water. This time there was the added problem of raw sewage. Under Royal Oak yard an old ceramic pipe had broken, spilling toilet contents directly into the brook, rather than into the sewer that runs underneath the stone floor. We weren't too happy about it, but we had come this far and had a mission to complete. I tried to remember not to bite my nails. We reached Adlington Square and could hear falling water. After letting everyone else go first, I nervously crawled into the lowest section yet – under an old stone arch, once a bridge over the open brook.

From the early seventeenth century until 1832 when it moved to Wellington Road, Stockport Grammar school was sited here – between 'School Brook' and Chestergate. The brook was crossed by the wooden Brook Bridge, which by 1744 was known as Schole-House Bridge. Boys fished in the brook by the school. At some point this stone bridge replaced the original. The Legh's of Adlington Hall also owned land here, with lush gardens, once the site of a sixteenth-century yarn croft. In the early eighteenth century they sold some of their land and Adlington Square, a right-angled street, was formed. Tin Brook's outfall between Chestergate (formerly Mersey) Tavern and the Primark (formerly Co-op) building was built in the mid-eighteenth century. In 1823, Thomas Ross' weaving and spinning factory, adjoining Adlington Square, had a waterwheel turned by the brook, with a fall of 20 feet, presumably into a wheel-pit as the natural fall is only around 10 feet.

On the south side of the bridge was the Briton's Protection public house, said to be a 'harbouring place for rogues, thieves, vagabonds, and prostitutes.' One Friday evening in

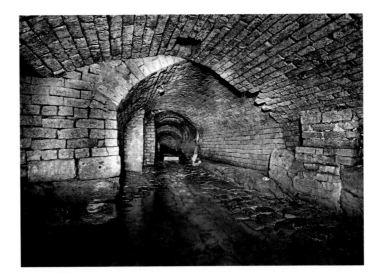

Tin Brook under
Lower Hillgate.

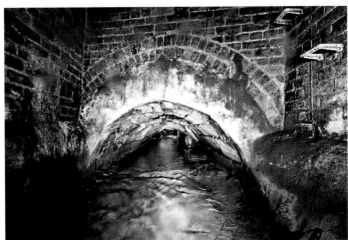

Schole-House
Bridge.

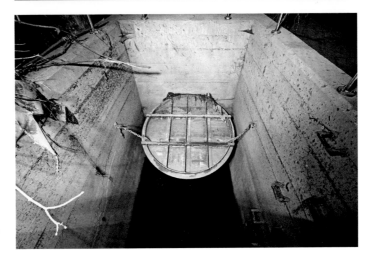

Tin Brook outlet to
the Mersey.

1823, a farmer, having sold his produce at the market, headed home with his earnings. He was seen to enter the Briton's Protection with a woman. He disappeared some time that evening. It was suggested he may have gone to the toilet in the backyard and fallen over the wall into Tin Brook. It had been raining and the water was high. On Saturday and Sunday men dragged the brook but found nothing. Then they searched the grid, which spanned the Mersey at Northenden, where they found his body with marks on it and his money and watch missing. The verdict was murder but no one was ever brought to justice.

At the end of the School Bridge section, two pieces of wood spanned a plughole, down which the brook splashes noisily. We leapt quickly over this unstable bridge. On the other side, rungs in the wall enabled us to go down 2 metres to the next level. The brook went north, to the right, and headed down a long RCP to its first outlet. We went to the left and found ourselves in a CSO. The 'fresh' flowed extremely fast in a narrow channel just a few feet below us.

In 1995 a new flood outlet sewer was built under Adlington Square to prevent storm water and sewage from backing up and Tin Brook's outfall was relocated farther to the east under Merseyway. Two large metal doors on the riverbank are designed to close when the Mersey rises. When the Mersey is above the level of the outlets, Tin Brook can fill the tunnel completely before it drains into the main sewer. It can be heard and seen through the grid near the entrance to the multistorey car park. The main sewer runs under Chestergate towards the treatment works at Cheadle. It was nothing like as big as we'd hoped and too small to be worth going in, much to my relief. We left the chamber by a second RCP, which we knew would lead to the second outlet. When we reached the end, the Mersey was quite high, lapping menacingly up to the door – an incoming tide of darkness. Should it rise much further we wouldn't be going back the same way, but we'd made it – Hempshaw Brook, from its source to its destination.

Railway Tunnels

The Cheshire Lines Committee (CLC) was formed by the joining of the Great Northern Railway (GNR) and the Manchester, Sheffield and Lincolnshire Railway (MS&LR) in 1865. They operated trains on the Godley to Skelton Junction line, which runs east–west through Stockport. It had one station (Tiviot Dale) and two goods yards (Portwood and Wellington Road) in the central Stockport area.

Tiviot Dale Station

The station opened in 1865 on the site of an old calico printing works. Originally named Stockport Teviot Dale, it changed to Stockport Tiviot Dale in 1874. The sign on the station building in a 1902 photograph says 'Cheshire Lines Tiviot Dale Station'. There were four lines, two each for through and local services. A fifth line went to an engine shed with a turntable and water tower, on the north side. The main station building was on the south (westbound) side of the tracks. There was also a building with a canopy on the north (eastbound) side.

The Prince of Wales (who would become King George V two years later) and his wife Mary visited Stockport in 1908 for the opening of the Town Hall. They arrived at Tiviot Dale station and were greeted by a guard of honour. Part of Heaton Lane was renamed Prince's Street for the route they took through Stockport.

The station closed in 1967 and demolition started in 1968. By 1969, all that was left was the westbound platform. The through lines remained in use for freight until 1980, but tracks were removed a few years later. Between Lancashire Hill flats and the motorway, hidden among trees and undergrowth, you can see the area where the station stood and the remains of the westbound platform.

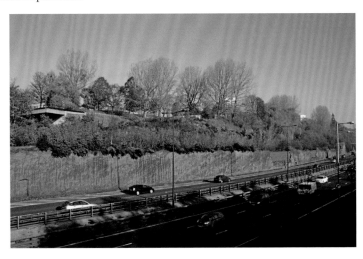

Tivot Dale railway cutting.

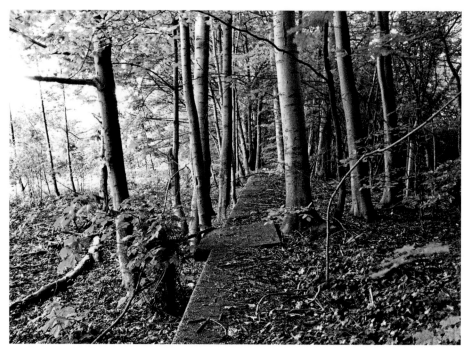

Tiviot Dale Station westbound platform.

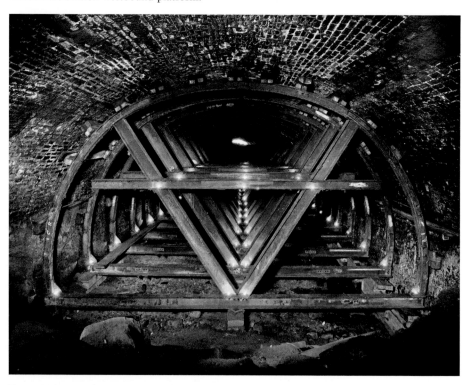

Tiviot Dale tunnel supporting girders.

West of the station, the CLC line ran through Tiviot Dale tunnel, then a deep cutting in the Heaton Norris hillside, then Wellington Road tunnel. During the construction of the 5.5 miles of line around Stockport, 403,000 cubic yards of rock were excavated and 35,000 cubic yards of stone and brickwork were laid. The land south of the cutting (which would later be removed to make way for the M60 motorway) sloped down towards Stockport. At the bottom stood tightly packed houses and small mills, including Throstle Grove Mill (a cotton spinning mill built in the 1810s, which by the 1820s was run by Ralph Orrell, of Travis Brow Mill). The name 'Throstle' comes from the throstle frame – a noisy spinning machine – and 'Grove' from the leafy hillside above the mill. The lost Stewart Street air-raid shelters extended into this hill, and partly underneath the railway cutting at the Wellington Road end.

Tiviot Dale Tunnel

Tiviot Dale Tunnel runs for nearly 150 metres, underneath the Christadelphian Meeting House and St Mary's Church car park. Lancashire Hill Bridge is over a short section of track at the start of the tunnel. If you stand on Lancashire Hill Bridge and look down at the ground by the rock face, you can just see the top of the tunnel's arch.

Dodge Hill air-raid shelters are squeezed into the ground between the railway tunnel and the buildings above, although not directly over the tunnel. During construction of the M60 a crane fell onto the hillside, damaging part of Dodge Hill shelter, though not the railway tunnel. Even so, as a precaution, a supporting framework of metal girders was installed in the tunnel and it was never to reopen.

Almost every local explorer has visited Tiviot Dale Tunnel. Its size and colours make for interesting photographs. On one trip, we met another group coming out – it's almost a tourist attraction. Both ends have been backfilled nearly to the top, but the centre section is full height. To reach it involved stooping and stumbling over dusty, sooty rubble. I held my hand to my face as I watched fine particles swirling around in my torch's beam. Reaching the end of the backfill I found myself atop an embankment with my head touching the blackened ceiling, looking along the full length of the tunnel towards a speck of green light from the western portal. A wide brick archway rose from the bedrock, soot-stained but

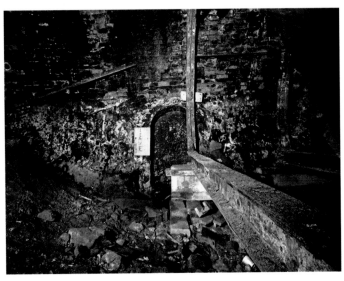

Niche in Tiviot Dale tunnel.

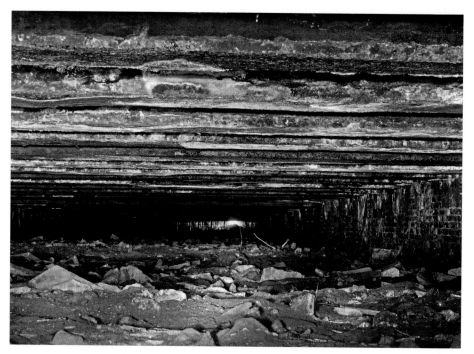

Looking towards the west portal of Wellington tunnel.

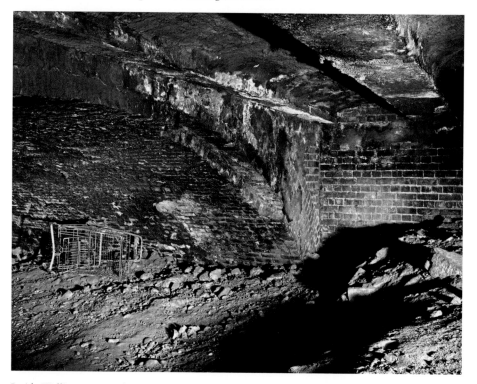

Inside Wellington tunnel.

intact. I slithered down to the bottom. My nose was hit with the smells of engine oil, fox urine, rotting wood and rusty iron. I clambered over girder after girder, past the red and yellow sandstones of Triassic pebble beds. Neat, person-sized alcoves are cut at intervals along the walls. We brought (and removed afterwards) 100 tea lights to place along the beams for a photograph. That wasn't nearly enough to cover every beam, but it was enough to light the foreground warmly.

Wellington Road Tunnel

Wellington Road Tunnel runs for around 220 metres underneath the A6, then Railway Street car park (formerly Kwik Save). Raised lettering on the lintel stone at the western portal reads '1864'. This can just be seen among the undergrowth behind Decathlon's outdoor display area.

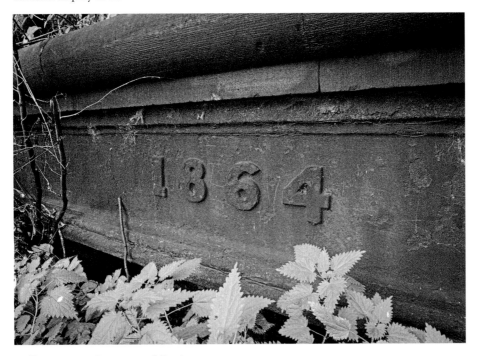

Wellington tunnel west portal lintel stone.

Air-Raid Shelters

The excavation of Stockport's air-raid shelters began in 1938. Engineers found that the optimal height to maximise capacity and minimise risk of collapse was 7 feet 6 inches, with a gentle arch. Using two pneumatic hand tools it took eight and a half hours to dig 3.5 feet, compared to just 9 inches when using rock picks. One yard of tunnel could hold four seated people and two standing. Stockport did suffer from bombardment and the shelters were well used, so much so that Chestergate shelter became known as the Chestergate Hotel. In 1948 all the shelters were sealed, with ventilating bricks at the entrances.

Brinksway

Brinksway air-raid shelter in Edgeley had the capacity for 1,083 bunks and 1,735 seats. It has a fairly straightforward layout: a main corridor follows the curves of the road, where there are five bricked-up entrance tunnels and a further three entrances are buried beneath the slope under Lark Hill Road. There were sixty-one toilets – scrap iron drums separated by canvas on timber frames – and twenty-five urinals. The total length of passages was 880 yards.

It was back in 2007 when I first visited Brinksway shelters. I was given directions to the entrance: go halfway up a steep, cobbled path, turn right into the woods, walk along a muddy trail, and drop into a hole in the ground. I found the hole. It had been broken through a concrete block, rusty reinforcing bars bent back. It was big enough for an average-sized person to slide through, with arms stretched above your head. I heard of one explorer, Bungle, who managed to squeeze in but couldn't get back out again and had to find an alternative exit. Living nearby, I spent a lot of time in Brinksway, showing friends around and having fun. Inevitably, the place deteriorated over the years; bed frames were broken up, rubbish left and fires started. The hole in the woods was capped again. Recently we discovered another way in, and decided to go back and take some proper photographs.

Dan and I entered from an unfamiliar direction, but we had plenty of lighting and I was confident we wouldn't get lost. We walked parallel to the road, peeping out through ventilation holes in the retaining wall to keep track of our location. All of the shelters are within the Chester Pebble Beds. Hard spring water has seeped between layers of rock, forming glistening sheets of colourful flowstone: deep blue azurite, a copper ore, and iridescent black, from cobalt or manganese. We found graffiti written by Alan Burgess, a Derbyshire Caving Club and Stockport Heritage member, who sadly passed away in 2011. Also known as 'Todge', Alan was a man I had only heard tell of, and wished I had met. He, Jim Clare, and Geoff Standring pioneered exploring Stockport's tunnels.

Chestergate

Chestergate was widened in 1938 and, when an old public house was demolished, it revealed wine cellars and domestic caves cut into the rock. The air-raid shelter used and

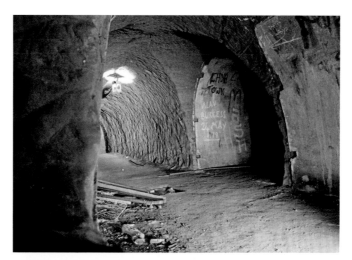

Brinksway air-raid shelter.

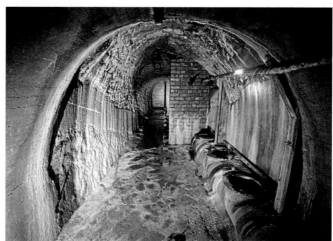

Brinksway air-raid shelter's toilets.

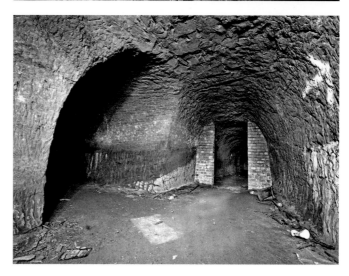

Dodge Hill air-raid shelter's tunnels.

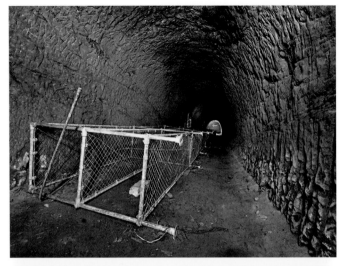

Dodge Hill air-raid shelter's beds.

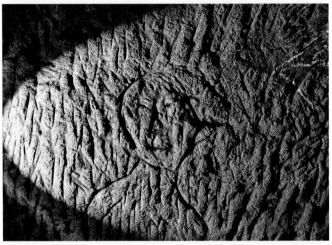

Carving in Dodge Hill air-raid shelter.

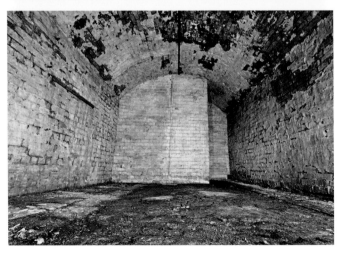

Ha'penny air-raid shelter.

expanded these cellars until it had the capacity for 6,500 people. It extends as far as Cooper's Brow and underneath St Peter's Church. One account tells of a boy being asked to take a message from the Chestergate end of the tunnels to the far side. The shelter was so packed he decided it was easier to go outside. The boy carefully put on his tin hat and ran along Chestergate and Underbank to the other entrance. Fortunately for him, no bombs fell and he delivered his message safely. Chestergate shelters are now open to the public and offer a fascinating tour through wartime Britain.

Dodge Hill

Dodge Hill air-raid shelter in Heaton Norris had the capacity for around 2,000 people. In recent years it has been sealed, then broken into several times. Homeless people slept there, teenagers got lost or set fires there. The access point was a small hole in the rock above the M60, narrow enough that you had to wiggle in sideways. Perhaps because of that, its artefacts remain relatively intact. The tunnels are neat and perfectly constructed. We found a couple of original decorations: a flower, and a person (pictured).

Stewart Street

Stewart Street air-raid shelter was in the hill sloping down to Great Egerton Street from Heaton Norris. It had four entrances: Gas Street (by the viaduct), Heaton Lane (behind the transport depot), Port Street (behind the Rock Inn), and Brown Street. During construction of the M60 in the 1980s a wide section of the hillside was cut away, taking with it the majority of the shelters. Workers found tunnels with beds and artefacts. It is assumed that the entire shelter has gone, however, I believe part of it still exists. Some of the tunnels on the 1940 survey extend farther north than the motorway. They may still be there, deep under Wellington Road and Railway Street car park.

Portwood

Harry told me there was also an air-raid shelter in Portwood. The National Archives refer to 'Underground accommodation: tunnel, Marsden Street, Portwood.' I think this may be what was once Marsland Street, on the wasteland next to Tesco. I know that a deep (4 metres below ground) sewer runs under there. There may also be remains of the Portwood cut and mills. At some point the land will be developed – it will be interesting to see what is uncovered.

Ha'penny

Back in 2010 I heard about an air-raid shelter next to Spring Mount Mill that may have connected to Brinksway shelter. I headed straight there only to arrive to find two men bolting a metal sheet to the entrance. They said I couldn't go in so I went home and forgot about it ... until recently, when Lee and I were looking to find a way into the now derelict mill. One evening, we clambered over the 4-metre-high gates, clanking noisily, and apparently drawing attention from vigilant neighbours. Running around the yard, we found that the whole mill was securely locked up. We left and walked back down

Brinksway, where we were stopped by a policeman driving up the hill. He had been called to the mill to investigate, so we told him it had indeed been us climbing the gates, we hadn't done any damage, and were sorry for having him called out. He was very nice and let us go about our business. We rejoined Dan, Bill and Matt, who had found that the air-raid shelter was now accessible.

Ha'penny shelter is an underground structure, with a baffle (staggered walls to reduce the effect of a bomb blast) between two large arched rooms. It is named for the handwritten message we found on the wall: 'Wilfred Halfpenny Friday Oct 1955 left the boys / weep'. At the western end is a rubble-filled opening, which we initially thought joined to Brinksway but could find no sign of a connection on the other side. Perhaps it was an exit, just another room.

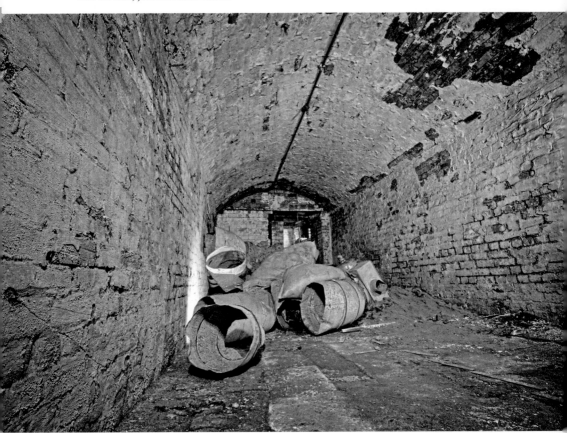

Ha'penny air-raid shelter.

Acknowledgements

Exploring Stockport has made for an interesting seven years. Every little piece of information I received was a new insight or trail to follow and, once known, impossible to ignore. I became 'a snapper-up of unconsidered trifles'. I am eternally grateful to the wonderful people who have accompanied or guided me along the way.

My huge thanks go to Daniel Dawson, Lee Price and Matt Brown – collectively known as the Stockport Historical Investigation Team – for making exploration fun as well as informative; Stockport Heritage Trust members, Jim Birch, Maureen Fahey, Marjorie Barlow, Steve Cliffe, Jill Trumble, Grace Collier, and Harry Pendlebury for their friendship and knowledge; Derbyshire Caving Club members, Geoff Standring, Bill Booth, Nigel Dibben, Edward Coghlan, Oliver King and Lauren Griffin for their advice, training, and helping to put it all into practice; Elle James, for encouragement and being my only hope of rescue should any of the many solo missions I undertook have gone wrong; Anne Forrester, Friends of Woodbank and Vernon Parks, for information about Woodbank Park tunnels; Ian Bell, Wheatley Plastics, for kind permission to visit Howard's Mill; Peter Arrowsmith, for some unexpected snippets of information; and to all of the friends who joined me for parts of the adventure: Simon, Zoe, Magda, Paco, Ewa, Maciej, Roybotnik, Monica, Lee, Kelly, Horus, Ojay, and Nickindroy.

Photograph credits: Thanks to Daniel Dawson for 'Merseyway looking east'; 'Merseyway looking west'; 'Beer Belly and The Ribcage', and to Lee Price for 'Carr Brook wheel-pit', 'Underneath Lower Carrs', and 'Carr Brook new pipe'.

Bibliography

Aiken, John, *A Description of the Country from Thirty to Forty Miles Round Manchester* (Cambridge University Press, 1795).

Arrowsmith, Peter, *Recording Stockport's Past* (Stockport Metropolitan Borough Council, 1996).

Arrowsmith, Peter, *Stockport: A History* (Stockport Metropolitan Borough Council, 1997).

Ashmore, Owen, *The Industrial Archaeology of Stockport* (University of Manchester, 1975).

Astle, William (ed.), *Centenary History of Stockport* (Swain and Co., 1922).

Baines, Edward, *History of the County Palatine and Duchy of Lancaster* (Fisher, Son and Co., 1836).

Blaikie, W. B., *The Scottish Historical Review,* Vol. VI, No. 23 (Edinburgh University Press, 1909).

Boyse, Samuel, *An Historical Review of the Transactions of Europe* (D. Henry, 1747).

British Geological Survey (Ordnance Survey, 1977).

Brown, Joshua, *Beating The Bounds* (Stockport Heritage Publications and Harcourt Brown, 1854).

Bulkeley, E. W., *Cheshire Notes and Queries* (Swain and Co. Ltd, 1886).

Chambers, Robert, *History of the Rebellion in Scotland in 1745, 1746*, Volume 1 (Edinburgh Printed for Constable, 1827).

Charles, George, *History of the Transactions in Scotland in the Years 1715–16*, Volumes 1–2 (J. Fisher and Co., 1816).

Chisholm, Hugh (ed.), *Encyclopaedia Britannica* (Encyclopaedia Britannica, Inc., 1911).

Cliffe, Steve, *Derbyshire Cavemen* (Amberley, 2010).

Cliffe, Steve, *Stockport Heritage Magazine* (Stockport Heritage Publications, 1996–2016).

Collier, Grace, *A Personal Journey Down The Tin Brook In Stockport* (Stockport Heritage Trust, 2006).

Crofton, Henry Thomas, *A History of the Ancient Chapel of Stretford in Manchester Parish v2* (Chetham Society, 1899).

Crofton, Henry Thomas, *Agrimensorial Remains around Manchester* (Lancashire and Cheshire Antiquarian Society, 1905).

De Rance, Charles E., *The Water Supply of England and Wales* (Edward Stanford, 1882).

Dranfield, Coral, *Rivers Under Your Feet* (Kevin Dranfield, 2006).

Farrer, William, *Lancashire Inquests Extents and Feudal Aids: v2 1310–1333* (The Record Society 1903–1915, 1907).

Gardner, W. & Whitaker E. C., *Tunnel Shelters in Stockport* (1940).

Goyt Valley Supply (Stockport Corporation Waterworks, 1937).

Great Britain Geological Survey and Museum, *Geology of the Country around Stockport and Knutsford* (Stationery Office Books, 1963).

'Greater Manchester Archaeological Unit', GMAU survey (GMAU, 2007).

Greville, M. D., *Chronology of the Railways of Lancashire* (Railway & Canal Historical Society, 1973).

Griffiths, K. J., Shand, P., & Ingram, J., *The Permo Triassic Sandstones of Manchester and East Cheshire* (British Geological Survey, 2003).

Hansard, Report from the select committee of the House of Lords – Pollution of Rivers Bill (1873 or 6).

Hanshall, J. H., *The History of the County Palatine of Chester* (G. Routledge, 1817).

Harrison, William, *Ancient Fords, Ferries, and Bridges in Lancashire* (Lancashire and Cheshire Antiquarian Society, 1897).

Heginbotham, Henry Thomas, *Stockport Ancient and Modern* (S. Low, Marston, Searle, & Rivington, 1877).

Homburg, E. & Travis, A. S. & Schröter, H. G., *The Chemical Industry in Europe, 1850–1914: Industrial Growth, Pollution, and Professionalization* (Kluwer Academic, 2013).

Hooley, James, Notes (Stockport Heritage Trust, 1970).

Hughes, Thomas (ed.), *Cheshire Sheaf* (The Cheshire Courant, 1878).

Johnson, William, *Map of Stockport*, (1820).

Journals of the House of Commons (House of Commons, 1793).

Kelsey, Charles E., *A History of Cheshire* (Oxford, 1911).

Kiernan, Mike, *Reddish Newtown – Life Below The Steps* (Mike Kiernan, 2005).

Leland, John, *Itinerary* (Lucy Toulmin 1906, 1535–1543).

Lewis, Samuel, A Topographical Dictionary of England (S Lewis & Co., 1835).

Long, George (ed.), *Penny Cyclopaedia* (Charles Knight, 1837).

Manley, Gordon, *The Mean Temperature of Central England 1698–1952* (Royal Meteorological Society, 1953).

Map of Roman Britain (Longmans Green and Co., 1910).

Marriot, Revd William, *Antiquities of Lyme and its Vicinity* (Oxford University, 1810).

Owens, Alastair John, *Small Fortunes: Property, Inheritance and the Middling Sort in Stockport* (University of London, 1800-1857).

Page, P. and Littlechilds, I., *River Mersey* (Amberley, 2014).

Parliament, Great Britain, 'The English Reports' (Volume 159) (House of Lords, 1900–1932).

Pigot, James, Pigot and Company's National Commercial Directory (Pigot and Co., 1828).

Pyne, W. H., *Lancashire Illustrated* (Henry Fisher, Son, and Jackson: London, 1831).

Record Society, *Lancashire Inquests, Extents, and Feudal Aids. Part II* (Kendal, 1879).

Remains, Historical & Literary, Connected with the Palatine Counties of Lancaster and Chester (Chetham Society, Manchester, 1844).

Smith, Dr Robert Angus, *Rivers Pollution Prevention Act 1876* (Hansard, 1881).

Stockdale, John, *Map of Environs of Mottram in Longendale* (John Stockdale, Piccadilly, 1794).

Stockport, Brinnington, *Edgeley and Brinksway Court of Requests County Cts.* (Lancashire and Cheshire Antiquarian Society, 1847).

Stopford, William, *A New and Accurate Map of the Environs of Stockport* (William Stopford, 1800).

The Stockport Book: Official Guide and Handbook (Metropolitan Borough of Stockport, 1991).

Various, Transactions (Lancashire and Cheshire Antiquarian Society, 1883–2012).

Watson, Revd John, *Archeologia or Miscellaneous Tracts Relating to Antiquity* (Society of Antiquaries of London, 1775).

Webb, William, *The Vale-royall of England; or the County Palatine of Chester* (Daniel King, 1621).

Westall, Roy, *Stockport: A Pictorial History* (Phillimore & Co. Ltd, 1988).

Whitaker, Revd John, *The History of Manchester: Saxon Period* (Joseph Johnson and J. Murray, 1775).